Strategic Intercessory Warfare I:
WEAPONS

Strategic Intercessory Warfare I:
WEAPONS

How to Be Equipped and Empowered

Through Spiritual Communications

Pauline Walley-Daniels, PhD.

Foreword: Dr. Kingsley Fletcher

XULON PRESS

Xulon Press
2301 Lucien Way #415
Maitland, FL 32751
407.339.4217
www.xulonpress.com

Unless otherwise indicated, Scripture quotations taken from the English Standard Version (ESV). Copyright © 2001 by Crossway, a publishing ministry of Good News Publishers. Used by permission. All rights reserved.

Scripture quotations taken from the King James Version (KJV) – public domain.

Scripture quotations taken from the New King James Version (NKJV). Copyright © 1982 by Thomas Nelson, Inc. Used by permission. All rights reserved.

Printed in the United States of America.

Paperback ISBN-13: 978-1-6312-9802-8

Ebook ISBN-13: 978-1-6312-9803-5

Table of Contents

Appendixes

Foreword

A s wisdom and understanding are dually critical variables in the equation of life, so is prayer and fasting to deliverance – each prompts the other to factor to its highest to yield the greatest result possible in the spirit realm. The book, **"Strategic Intercessory Warfare: Weapons"** penned by Dr. Pauline Walley-Daniels, is an incomparable manual on how to effectively experience true freedom in Christ Jesus and help others in the same.

Dr. Walley-Daniels' writings are always timely, deeply reflective, and provoking; and understood by clergy and lay-people alike. Her latest work continues in this vein, yet on a higher scale and thus is destined to be an even greater blessing to the Body of Christ.

I highly recommend incorporating the principles of ", **"Strategic Intercessory Warfare: Weapons"** in your daily life and in the Prayer and Intercessory ministries of your church. You will be amazed at the impact of its teaching!

Dr. Kingsley Fletcher
Founder and Overseer
Life International
Research Triangle, North Carolina, USA

Introduction

Strategic Intercessory Warfare

N**O military officer goes** to war without weapons. No commander-in-chief sends out a troop of army officers without training them to identify wars and how to face battles. No officer carries a weapon that he has not been trained to handle.

More often than not, many people go to war without identifying their enemy. Once they sense an attack, they pick up their artilleries and start to shoot randomly without mapping out the direction of the target or finding out the root cause of the matter. There are so many questions to be asked and answered before embarking on a war or a retaliation mission. Some of the important questions include:

- What triggered the attack?
- Who is involved?
- What must I do to stop the war?
- Why should I counter the attack?
- Who is the enemy in this case?
- How and when should I retaliate if necessary?

This book, *Strategic Intercessory Warfare I: Weapons, How to be Equipped and Empowered through Spiritual*

Communication, educates you on how to go into the presence of God your Father. It enlightens you on how to identify a particular problem that needs to be solved, and what kind of weapon is needed for a specific warfare. It also enables you to understand the kind of preparation that is needed to gather information from the realms of the spirit into the natural.

Intercession in Action

Prayer Focus
Ability to Map out the Target of War

Goal
Ability to discover the root cause of the war;
Need to know the particular enemy behind the war;
Need wisdom to counter the enemy;
Need divine instruction and direction to conquer the
enemy at stake.

Prayer of Confession and Repentance
O Lord, I confess the weaknesses and mistakes that have
opened the door for the enemy to attack me and family.
O Lord, I am sorry that I have not observed your laws and
statutes, and as a result, the enemy has gained a loophole into
my environment to attack us.

Prayer of Forgiveness and Restoration
O Lord, I plead forgiveness, and ask for the blood of Jesus to
wash and cleanse us from all ungodliness.
O Lord, consider your grace and mercies, as your promised
to forgiven whenever we repent from our sins.
O Lord, forgive and restore us into fellowship with you,
That the enemy will no longer gain advantage over us.

Plea for Divine Intervention
Jehovah God, you are the God of Mercy;
You are the Compassionate One that forgives;
O Lord, intervene in this case,
And show me what you want me to do,
In order to conquer the enemy.
O Lord, remember how you directed Joshua in the battle
against Ai and the enemies of Israel;
O Lord, remember how you fought the battle for Israel,

In a manner that caused the surrounding nations to
fear you, God.
So let it be my portion, that you will fight my battles,
And you will cause my enemies to know that you are
Jehovah El Gibbor -
The Might Warrior.

Invocation of Blessings

O Lord, bless me with your favor
And cause your face to shine upon me;
O Lord, surround me with your fire of protection,
And consume the arrows of divination,
And the terror of darkness that rise up against me;
O Lord, Bless me with your grace,
So that I will not be destroyed by the workers of iniquity.
Thank you, Lord, for granting me your grace and mer-
cies. Amen.

Chapter One

The Realms of Prayer

The Season of Rest

I n **the later months** of every year, I usually spend time seeking the Lord for a mandate for the upcoming year. Also, in the beginning of the year, I continue to seek the Lord for the details of that particular year's mandate. This manner of seeking is to enable me to hear and understand divine instructions directing my path for the year. I do not like to copy the way anybody does anything. I prefer to consult with the Lord my maker. An act may appear beautiful and attractive, but it may not be the pattern that the Lord might want me to adopt. God is on the minority side of events. It is better to do things in a unique way that identifies with you, rather than copycatting things that are not meant to fulfill your destiny. **Matthew 6:31-33 (KJV)** says,

> Therefore take no thought, saying, What shall we eat? or, What shall we drink? or, Wherewithal shall we be clothed? (For after all these things do the Gentiles seek:) for your heavenly Father knoweth that ye have need of all these things. But *seek ye first the kingdom of God, and his*

1

righteousness; and all these things shall be added unto you.

In view of the fact that I believe that I am on divine assignment on earth, I endeavor to strive for the wishes of my Father God in heaven in order to walk and live in obedience to his will. In order to understand the progression of this discussion, it is necessary to define the term *mandate* in this regard.

Divine Mandate: Divine Mandate is a specific assignment for a particular season that the Lord has set up for an individual, a people, a place, or an organization. It can be defined as such:

- It is an official command or instruction to perform an assignment.
- It is an order from a higher authority from above—the throne of the Almighty God.
- It is a divine commission to administrate an assignment involving other people or an organization.

Rest: During the year of 2015, the Lord encouraged us to rest. Hence, I wrote a series of articles on the need to rest—to observe the act of rest as stated in the Ten Commandments, and also as a requirement to rejuvenate the human body system.

In view of the fact that it was part of the natural system that the Lord had laid down for mankind from the beginning of creation, it is very important to rest, as God himself observed the act on the seventh day of creation. I discovered that many untimely, premature, and accidental deaths were caused by lack of rest.

As a minister involved in constant spiritual warfare in order to carry out effective deliverance ministration, there was the need to ensure that all doors and windows were properly closed and locked against any form of invasion from the camp of the enemy. Besides, physical and spiritual doors are usually controlled by emotional, financial, and other environmental activities that could create a loophole for the enemy to enter through familiarity and carelessness.

Call to Intercede: In 2015, while the Lord ordered us to rest from war, he also mandated us to come into fellowship with him through intercessory prayer. This instruction meant that, instead of fighting wars, we were going to turn over our burdens and battles to the Holy Spirit, while we spent the time in a personal relationship with him. "So Joshua took the whole land, according to all that the LORD said unto Moses; and Joshua gave it for an inheritance unto Israel according to their divisions by their tribes. And the land rested from war" (**Joshua 11:23**).

This kind of intercessory prayer fellowship is to draw us closer into a relationship that could be described as such:

- It is the state of the bride in the arms of the groom.
- It is a leisure time between a child and the father— Father-daughter/Father-son relationship
- It is a state of relaxation to experience the joy of salvation.
- It is a time of receiving rewards and compensation from some efforts invested.
- It is time for recovery and restoration.

As the Lord spoke to me, my understanding was enlightened; as this divine mandate caused me to understand another meaning of intercessory prayer, beyond making an appeal in the court of heaven.

- Intercessory prayer in one realm is a romantic affair between a bride and a groom.
- Intercessory prayer in another realm is also a heart-to-heart talk between a parent and a child.

- Intercessory prayer in another realm is a key that opens an uncommon door for favor.
- Intercessory prayer in another realm gives the power to reverse unfavorable decisions to become favorable before the laws on earth.
- Intercessory prayer grants one access into the throne room of heaven and the place of earthly kingdoms.

Wow! This is awesome! Immediately, I was swung into the spirit realm to watch an interesting movie. The scenario was an excerpt from the biblical book of Esther. I watched how Esther used her romantic love to intercede for her people and to deliver the Jewish race from the hand of the wicked Haman. Haman had secured an edict from King Ahasuerus to annihilate the Jews throughout the Persian kingdom. By divine intervention, Esther acquired a unique wisdom that enabled her to win the heart of the king. Hence, the Jews gained an international freedom from Haman's destruction. Thus, the matter was reversed on behalf of Esther and the Jewish race (**Esther 5-6**).

The Blood of Prayer

The language of prayer runs through my family's bloodline, as it seems to make up 99 percent of our DNA and 100 percent of my personal life. Prayer is my live wire. It is the unique carrier of genetic information that fills my heart—body, soul, and spirit. Every moment of my thought is a conversation with the Lord. I am always asking the Lord what to do, when to do, and how to do? Seeking to know his designed plan and purpose for my daily endeavors is the utmost desire of my life. "Thy will be done on earth as it is in heaven" (**Matthew 10:10 KJV**).

I am the firstborn of seven children—three ladies and four gentlemen. When we were growing up as little children, our parents used to wake us up early in the morning by 5:00 a.m. for morning devotion, to read the Bible and pray. As part of the morning devotion, our routine assignments were dealt out to us with consciousness of what the Almighty God our Creator expected of us. With this kind of instruction and direction, the fear of God was implanted into every activity concerning our daily endeavors. We were made to understand that we could not do anything without offering prayer to God for direction and protection.

In fact, our parents demonstrated the need to make a connection with the Lord before touching or doing anything. Before stepping out of the house, my parents would go behind the door to say a word of prayer. When they returned home from wherever they went, they would first of all enter the living room or bedroom and offer appreciative prayer unto the Lord for safely returning home before sharing pleasantries with anyone. It was almost an abomination to say a greeting before you gave thanks to the Lord. Prayer was offered before and after meals. Prayer was also said at night before we went to bed. So, the day started with prayer and the evening was rounded up with a word of prayer of thanksgiving. As commonly said, "Jesus started with prayer and ended with prayer."

Spiritual Communication

Prayer is communication between man and God. It is also a call upon the Almighty God. For non-Christians, prayer may be a call upon a deity, a spirit, an idol, or anything that one believes in or refers to as god. However, in this book, *all discussions focus on the realms of Christianity and the Christian mode of prayers*. Therefore, from the Christian perspective, prayer can be given different types of definitions from a biblical background.

- Fundamentally, prayer is the spiritual communication between man and God.
- It is the type of communication that allows mankind to relate to God in terms of a relationship, where one expects a response after speaking.

- It is the process of interaction where one experiences feedback as in the state of conversation between two or more people.
- Precisely, communication with the Almighty God is two-way traffic.

The Intention of Prayer: Furthermore, prayer is a spiritual dialogue that has the power to change situations. Besides that, the actual intention of prayer is to feel the presence of the Lord. Also, it is to receive the supply to our needs, which may result in effective dialogue, whereby the Almighty God manifests himself on earth as purposed in heaven. Thus, we are able to enter into the mode of spiritual communication, whenever we open our mouth to speak to the Lord, to discuss a matter with him, or bring a case before him. As stated in the Lord's Prayer, **"Thy kingdom comes. Thy will be done in earth, as it is in heaven. Give us this day our daily bread. And forgive us our debts, as we forgive our debtors"** (**Matthew 6:10-12 KJV**).

Monologue Type of Prayer

Lack of Attention: When people do not have an attentive ear, their prayers tend to become a monologue conversation. Thus, prayer is consciously or unconsciously considered as a one-way type of traffic that does not accommodate an exchange or response in communication.

Lack of Patience: There is a tendency for some people to do all the talking in prayer as though the Almighty God does not have the ability to respond to anything that they have said. Some people do not have the patience and the ability to listen to the Lord's response, nor to other people even in a face-to-face conversation. That kind of attitude makes it seem as though prayer is one-way traffic, but it is not so. It also makes it sound as if God is unapproachable or does not have the time to listen to whatever we have to say to him; but that notion is not correct.

Overwhelming Challenges: Sometimes when people are saddled with mountains of problems, they rarely pay attention to anything, except the burden of challenges or difficulties on their hearts and shoulders. They may attempt to listen to some, or all kinds of advice, yet they may not hear anything being said to them. Most times, when people come to our office for counseling, I realize that the best thing to do is to allow them to pour out their hearts. I also allow them to cry and boil so that every pain in their heart, mind, and soul is released until their expression is turned into a smile or laughter. Usually, unless a person seeking counseling is allowed to speak out his or her mind and pour out whatever acid is boiling in their belly, they will not be able to take in whatever you have for them as advice or correction.

Lack of Understanding the Problem: Note that you can only make intercession for a case that has been presented to you. You need to pay attention to the person seeking your help. So, the initial part of the counseling session may seem as though you are in a monologue for about an hour or more, depending on the type of case.

The Cycle of Events: Similarly, some people go into the presence of God with the same type of attitude. To such individuals, they need someone to listen to them. In view of their need, their hearts desire may sound like this: *"Please Lord, just listen to what I have to say to you. I just need somebody to listen to me."*

Prayer Is Attention Oriented: Prayer is attention oriented. It demands that we make the time to be in the presence of God the Father, just as we pay attention to our loved ones, and other activities that are considered very important in our lives.

Every relationship demands some kind of attention. A relationship between God our Father and mankind is very much demanding and must be given first and special priority in our lives. It is very important to reverence the Almighty God as our Father, who created us for a purpose. Therefore, we need to consider his perfect will in all that we say or do in our life's endeavors. His purpose must supersede our personal desires and wishes. We can only know his will when we stay in his presence attentively. More so, we must learn to listen for a response any time we speak to him, bearing in mind that communication with the Father is two-way traffic. God listens and answers when we call upon Him. **Jeremiah 33:2-3** declares,

> Thus says the LORD who made the earth, the LORD who formed it to establish it—the LORD is his name: **"Call** to me and I will answer you, and will tell you great and hidden things that you have not known."

Some of the biblical personalities who had effective communication with the Almighty God, as they paid attention to his voice to follow divine instructions and directives, included:

- Noah for the building of the ark
- Abraham to raise a nation of faith
- Moses to lead Israel to the Promised Land
- Joshua to establish Israel in the Promised Land

Each of these individuals paid special attention to the Almighty God with reverence, honor, and respect. Besides, they asked questions whenever they needed clarification on what to do and sought his will until they understood divine instructions.

Father Noah Heard and Obeyed the Lord

Father Noah was a disciplined listener, who heard the voice of the Lord and was able to receive detailed instructions. He followed divine directions to build the ark that preserved the lives of his household during the era of the flood. **Genesis 6:11-22** says,

> Now the earth was corrupt in God's sight, and the earth was filled with violence. And God saw the earth, and behold, it was corrupt, for all flesh had corrupted their way on the earth. And God said to Noah, "I have determined to make an end of all flesh, for the earth is filled with violence through them. Behold, I will destroy them with the earth. Make yourself an ark of gopher wood. Make rooms in the ark, and cover it inside and out with pitch. This is how you are to make it: the length of the ark 300 cubits, its breadth 50 cubits, and its height 30 cubits. Make a roof for the ark, and finish it to a cubit above, and set the door of the ark in its side. Make it with lower, second, and third decks. For behold, I will bring a flood of waters upon the earth to destroy all flesh in which is the breath of life under heaven. Everything that is on the earth shall die. But I will establish my covenant with you, and you shall come into the ark, you, your sons, your wife, and your sons' wives with you. And of every living thing of all flesh, you shall bring two of every sort into the ark to keep them alive with you. They shall be male and female. Of the birds according to their kinds, and of the animals according to their kinds, of every creeping thing of the ground, according to its kind, two of every sort shall come in to you to keep them alive. Also take with you every sort of food that is eaten, and store it up. It shall serve as food for you and for them." Noah did this; he did all that God commanded him.

Genesis 7:1-7,

> Then the LORD said to Noah, "Go into the ark, you and all your household, for I have seen that you are righteous before me in this generation. Take with you seven pairs of all clean animals, the male and his mate, and a pair of the animals that are not clean, the male and his mate, and seven pairs of the birds of the heavens also, male and female, to keep their offspring alive on the face of all the earth. For in seven days I will send rain on the earth forty days and forty nights, and every living thing that I have made I will blot out from the face of the ground." And Noah did all that the LORD had commanded him. Noah was six hundred years old when the flood of waters came upon the earth. And Noah and his sons and his wife and his sons' wives with him went into the ark to escape the waters of the flood.

Father Abraham Heard and Obeyed the Lord

Communion: Father Abraham had the opportunity to commune with the Lord. He also had the opportunity to bargain with the Lord concerning his nephew Lot.

Voice Recognition: Firstly, Abraham recognized the voice of the Almighty God and respected divine instructions. So the Lord testified to that effect thus in, **Genesis 26:5** "Abraham obeyed my voice and kept my charge, my commandments, my statutes and my laws."

Humility: Secondly, Abraham respected and feared the Lord. He humbled himself as he bowed during a conversation that related to his heart's desire for a son - **Genesis 17: 17-19, 21,**

Then Abraham fell on his face and laughed and said to himself, "Shall a child be born to a man who is a hundred years old? Shall Sarah, who is ninety years old, bear a child?" And Abraham said to God, "Oh that Ishmael might live before you!" God said, "No, but Sarah your wife shall bear you a son, and you shall call his name Isaac. I will establish my covenant with him as an everlasting covenant for his offspring after him. But I will establish my covenant with Isaac, whom Sarah shall bear to you at this time next year."

Negotiation: Thirdly, Abraham had a discussion with the Lord over the destruction of Sodom and Gomorrah in **Genesis 18:19-30**,

For I have chosen him, that he may command his children and his household after him to keep the way of the LORD by doing righteousness and justice, *so that the LORD may bring to Abraham what he has promised him.*" Then the LORD said, *"Because the outcry against Sodom and Gomorrah is great and their sin is very grave,* I will go down to see whether they have done altogether according to the outcry that has come to me. And if not, I will know."

So the men turned from there and went toward Sodom, but *Abraham still stood before the LORD*. Then Abraham drew near and said, *"Will you indeed sweep away the righteous with the wicked? Suppose* there are fifty righteous within the city. Will you then sweep away the place and not spare it for the fifty righteous who are in it? Far be it from you to do such a thing, to put the righteous to death with the wicked, so that the righteous fare as the wicked! *Far be that from you! Shall not the Judge of all the earth do what is just?" And the LORD said,* "If I find at Sodom fifty righteous in the city, I will spare the whole place for their sake." *Abraham answered and said,* "Behold, I have undertaken to speak to the Lord, I who am but dust and ashes. Suppose five of the fifty righteous are lacking. Will you destroy the whole city for lack of five?" And he said, "I will not destroy it if I find forty-five there." *Again he spoke to him and said,* "Suppose forty are found there." He answered, "For the sake of forty I will not do it." *Then he said,* "Oh let not the Lord be angry, and I will speak. Suppose thirty are found there." He answered, "I will not do it, if I find thirty there." *He said,* "Behold, I have undertaken to speak to the Lord. Suppose twenty are found there." He answered, "For the sake of twenty I will not destroy it." *Then he said,* "Oh let not the Lord be angry, and I will speak again but this once. Suppose ten are found there." He answered, "For the sake of ten I will not destroy it." And the LORD went his way, when he had finished speaking to Abraham, and Abraham returned to his place.

Access: As a friend of God, Abraham enjoyed a good relationship and also had access to him.

Isaiah 41:8 But you, Israel, my servant, Jacob, whom I have chosen, the offspring of Abraham, my friend.

James 2:23 And the Scripture was fulfilled that says, "Abraham believed God, and it was counted to him as righteousness"—and he was called a friend of God.

Father Jacob Heard and Obeyed

Just like his grandfather Abraham, Jacob had a conversational encounter with the Lord on a few occasions.

Genesis 32:30 So Jacob called the name of the place Peniel, saying, *"For I have seen God face to face, and yet my life has been delivered."*

Moses Heard and Obeyed

Moses had one of the best accesses into the presence of the Lord and had various forms of communication with him without any hindrance. He was frequently in and out of the presence of the Lord as he asked, sought, and knocked on the doors of his chambers. He allowed the Lord to be his director and instructor in every realm of his endeavors, irrespective of his weaknesses and mistakes. Moses was human, and humans do err. Nevertheless, he allowed the Lord to be the ruler of his destiny.

Exodus 33:11 Thus the LORD used to speak to Moses face to face, as a man speaks to his friend. When Moses turned again into the camp, his assistant Joshua the son of Nun, a young man, would not depart from the tent.

Deuteronomy 34:10 And there has not arisen a prophet since in Israel like Moses, whom the LORD knew face to face.

Numbers 14:14 And they will tell the inhabitants of this land. They have heard that you, O LORD, are in the midst of this people. For you, O LORD, are seen face to face, and your cloud stands over them and you go before them, in a pillar of cloud by day and in a pillar of fire by night.

Deuteronomy 5:4 The LORD spoke with you face to face at the mountain, out of the midst of the fire,

Joshua Heard and Obeyed

Joshua's relationship and service to Moses gave him the opportunity to inherit a unique legacy of leadership. Hence, he gained communicative access into the presence of the Lord. When Israel fell into the hands of their enemy because of one man's contamination of the camp, Joshua sought the Lord. Some of the conversation that ensued between him and the Lord is recorded in **Joshua 7:6-10**,

> Then Joshua tore his clothes and fell to the earth on his face before the ark of the LORD until the evening, he and the elders of Israel. And they put dust on their heads. *And Joshua said,* "Alas, O Lord GOD, why have you brought this people over the Jordan at all, to give us into the hands of the Amorites, to destroy us? Would that we had been content to dwell beyond the Jordan! *O Lord, what can I say,* when Israel has turned their backs before their enemies! For the Canaanites and all the inhabitants of the land will hear of it and will surround us and cut off our name from the earth. *And what will you do for your great name?" The LORD said*

to Joshua, "Get up! Why have you fallen on your face?

Other Prophets Heard and Obeyed

Most of the biblical prophets (major and minor prophets) like Samuel, Elijah, Elisha, Daniel, Isaiah, Ezekiel, Hosea, Amos, and Joel were men who had open access into the presence of the Almighty God. They heard him clearly, as they were able to receive instructions and directions on behalf of the people and the nations in which they dwelt. These categories of people were referred to as prophets because they were able to have detailed communication with the Lord.

> **Judges 6:22** Then Gideon perceived that he was the angel of the LORD. And Gideon said, "Alas, O Lord GOD! For now I have seen the angel of the LORD face to face."

Friendship with God

Jesus said in **John 15:14-16,**

> *You are my friends if you do what I command you.* No longer do I call you servants, for the servant does not know what his master is doing; but I have called you friends, for all that I have heard from my Father I have made known to you. You did not choose me, but I chose you and appointed you that you should go and bear fruit and that your fruit should abide, so that whatever you ask the Father in my name, he may give it to you.

Intercession in Action

Prayer Focus
Understand the Realms of Prayer

Goal
Need to understand the realms of prayer
Need to know how to intercede
Need to know how to seek the Lord through intercessory prayer
Need to be attentive to divine instruction and direction

Prayer of Worship
O Lord our God and Maker,
The great and awesome God.
The Covenant Keeping God,
Whose steadfast love never ceases,
The God who watches over his commands,
O Lord, let your ears be attentive to our cry.
And hear the cry of our hearts,
As we call upon you day and night.

Prayer of Confession and Repentance
O Lord, listen to the confession of our sins,
Which we have sinned against you.
We confess and repent from our trespasses
As our fathers and mothers from many generations
Have transgressed your Word
by committing grievous sins against your commands.
We have acted corruptly against you
And have not kept your laws,
The statutes, and the rules according to your written Word.
O Lord, remember your Word that states in 1 John 1:9 that,
"If we confess our sins, [you are] faithful and just to forgive us
our sins and to cleanse us from all unrighteousness."

O Lord, please forgive us our sins,
And restore us unto yourself.

Prayer of Forgiveness and Restoration:
O Lord, remember your word in Joel 2:12-13 that also
states that,
"'Yet even now," declares the LORD,
'return to me with all your heart,
with fasting, with weeping, and with mourning;
and rend your hearts and not your garments.'
Return to the LORD your God,
for he is gracious and merciful,
slow to anger, and abounding in steadfast love;
and he relents over disaster."
O Lord, forgive and remove the affliction of sin out
of our lives
According to your written word in Joel 2:20 (KJV) that says,
"But I will remove far off from you
the northern army, and will drive him into a land
barren and desolate, with his face toward the east sea,
and his hinder part toward the utmost sea,
and his stink shall come up, and his ill savour shall come up,
because he hath done great things."
O Lord, remember your promise for restoration according to
Joel 2:19,
"The LORD answered and said to his people,
'Behold, I am sending to you
grain, wine, and oil,
and you will be satisfied;
and I will no more make you
a reproach among the nations."

Petition
O Lord, I need to understand the realms of prayer;
Teach me to make intercession in your presence;

O Lord, teach me to how to seek your will, that I may know
your plans and purposes;
O Lord, enable me to be attentive to divine instruction and
direction,
so that I may walk in obedience to your Word.

Invocation of Blessings
O Lord, open the windows of heaven
and pour out your blessings unto us according to
Joel 2:22-27,
""""Fear not, …
for the pastures of the wilderness are green;
the tree bears its fruit;
the fig tree and vine give their full yield.
"Be glad, O children of Zion,
and rejoice in the LORD your God,
for he has given the early rain for your vindication;
he has poured down for you abundant rain,
the early and the latter rain, as before.
The threshing floors shall be full of grain;
the vats shall overflow with wine and oil.
I will restore to you the years that the swarming locust
has eaten,
the hopper, the destroyer, and the cutter, my great army,
which I sent among you.
"You shall eat in plenty and be satisfied,
and praise the name of the LORD your God,
who has dealt wondrously with you.
And my people shall never again be put to shame.
You shall know that I am in the midst of Israel,
and that I am the LORD your God and there is none else."

Song of Motivation

Draw Me Nearer (Crosby)
Frances J. Crosby, pub. 1875
Copyright status is *Public Domain*
Subject: Supplication
Scripture: Jeremiah 30:21-22; Hebrews 10:22

1. I am Thine, O Lord, I have heard Thy voice,
   And it told Thy love to me;
   But I long to rise in the arms of faith
   And be closer drawn to Thee.

   Refrain: Draw me nearer, nearer blessed Lord,
   To the cross where Thou hast died;
   Draw me nearer, nearer, nearer blessed Lord,
   To Thy precious, bleeding side.

2. Consecrate me now to Thy service, Lord,
   By the pow'r of grace divine;
   Let my soul look up with a steadfast hope,
   And my will be lost in Thine.

3. Oh, the pure delight of a single hour
   That before Thy throne I spend,
   When I kneel in prayer, and with Thee, my God
   I commune as friend with friend!

4. There are depths of love that I cannot know
   Till I cross the narrow sea;
   There are heights of joy that I may not reach
   Till I rest in peace with Thee.

Reference:
www.BibleResources.org
www.library.timelesstruths.org/music/
Draw_Me_Nearer_Crosby/

Chapter Two

The Nature of Prayer

The Characteristics of Prayer: Besides being a type of spiritual communication, prayer has a peculiar nature. In its characteristics, prayer is invocation, devotion, orison, and intercession. This chapter focuses on the nature of certain types of spiritual communication that could be classified as intercessory prayers, because they are usually pronounced and declared on behalf of a people.

Invocation

nvocation is the act of demonstrating respect and honor to the Almighty God by inviting his presence into a gathering at the beginning of a ceremony such as a worship service, a meeting, and/or a fellowship. It is a process of quoting Scripture verses or laws as the legal grounds to make utterances in the name of the Lord, or in the name of a deity (such as Satan or demon gods/idols) to justify one's intention.

Also, invocation is to make declarations and decrees. It is the act of pronouncing blessings or curses upon a person/people, a place, or a thing.

Invocation is usually pronounced at the beginning of a meeting.

Regular Invocation

Invite the presence of the Lord into a meeting from the beginning in a form of opening prayer or invocation. An invocation usually starts with an announcement:

Let us Pray

> Great God of Wonders, we praise and give thanks to thee for giving us the opportunity to gather here for today's fellowship.
>
> O Lord, we ask for thy Holy Spirit to fill us as you did in the days of the apostles on the day of Pentecost.
>
> O Lord, we ask for wisdom, knowledge, skillfulness, and understanding in all aspects of our discussion that your perfect will would permeate every decision that we make in this gathering today.
>
> Let thy will be done on earth as it is in heaven according to thy Word in the Lord's prayer as it is written in **Matthew 6:10**, *"Thy kingdom come, thy will be done on earth as it is in heaven."*

Wedding Invocation

An invocation is usually pronounced at the start and end of a wedding ceremony, as soon as the bride arrives to receive the blessing of being joined together with the groom. The Almighty God is invited according to biblical truth and petition is made to grant the newly wedded couple the grace and endurance to establish their marriage on the platform of everlasting love.

Let Us Pray

Almighty and Everlasting God, our gracious Father, we give thanks to you for granting us life and strength to witness the wedding ceremony between our brother, _____ and sister _____.

We ask for your divine grace and sanction upon this marriage.

O Lord, release your blessings upon these vows of commitment as they become one bone and one flesh.

O Lord, enable their body, soul, and spirit to be united for life as in the trinity.

Incantation

Incantation depicts a negative influence of summoning demons or evil spirits into action, while invocation carries a positive intention of inviting the presence of the Lord God into a place or ceremony.

An incantation is a language of enchantment spoken, written, or sung in a rhyme to conjure evil spirits and powers of darkness, and also summon them into action. It is a ritual citation of words that have magical effect to manifest an intended evil.

It is a form of casting spells or calling for the appearance of evil spirits. It is the words and language spoken during the ritual process of casting spells. The spell is the ritual of sacrifice that may involve the shedding of blood, burning of candles, herbs, and other forms of items as required in a specific situation. Incantations are the words that the workers of iniquity utter as evil or satanic prayers.

Incantations are also known as enchantments, bewitchment, charms, conjurations, hexes, spells, whammies, etc.

Incantations are made during ritual services to invoke the presence of evil spirits such as witchcraft, magic, occultism, shamanism, voodoo, etc. It is used to charm a person, a people, a place or a thing.

- An incantation is a magical enchantment.
- It is a magical ceremony.
- It is an act of witchcraft.
- Magic is also known as black magic and wizardry.

Balak, the king of Moab, employed the services of a magician called Balaam to curse the people of Israel during the days of their wilderness journey to the Promised Land. The episode that ensued in the event of the Balaam's enchantment is recorded in the book of **Numbers 23:7-12, 23**,

> And Balaam took up his discourse and said, "From Aram Balak has brought me, the king of Moab from the eastern mountains: 'Come, curse Jacob for me, and come, denounce Israel!'
>
> How can I curse whom God has not cursed? How can I denounce whom the LORD has not denounced? For from the top of the crags I see him, from the hills I behold him; behold, a people dwelling alone, and not counting itself among the nations! Who can count the dust of Jacob or number the fourth part of Israel? Let me die the death of the upright, and let my end be like his!"
>
> And Balak said to Balaam, "What have you done to me? I took you to curse my enemies, and behold, you have done nothing but bless

them." And he answered and said, "Must I not take care to speak what the LORD puts in my mouth?"

For there is no enchantment against Jacob, no divination against Israel; now it shall be said of Jacob and Israel, 'What has God wrought!'

Incantations are meant to command evil and to cast spells. Sometimes, people who were once involved in the act of incantation have imported the procedure into the Christian system of prayers. In recent times, many prayers offered in churches are similar to incantation as death sentences are passed on fellow brothers and sisters considered as enemies. It is awful to hear the chanting of evil spells being cast against one another in "the name of Jesus," while the gospel of truth commands us to use good to overcome evil. Note what **Luke 6:43, 45** says,

"For no good tree bears bad fruit, nor again does a bad tree bear good fruit ...

The good person out of the good treasure of his heart produces good, and the evil person out of his evil treasure produces evil, for out of the abundance of the heart his mouth speaks.

How can we propagate the gospel truth to save souls when we pronounce destruction on the people that we are supposed to rescue from perishing?

According to *www.sacredtext.com* the nature of an incantation includes the following:

- Incantation is a command
- It is a chant
- It is repeated until the impact is felt
- It is uttered with an under-voice.

- The language and wording must be exact.
- The aim is to secure a targeted evil.
- The name of Almighty God is not involved.

Devotion

Devotion is an act of spending time with the Lord God. It is an expression of deep love and commitment to the Lord. It is a sense of loyalty and attachment that shows dedication to the relationship that exists between a person and the Lord. It is a unique passion that one has towards prayer in view of developing one's relationship with the Lord.

Devotion is a means of developing an intimate relationship through Bible reading and praying. Spending special time with the Lord on a daily basis helps to build up one's faith, and to strengthen one's relationship with the Creator.

> **James 4:7-8** Submit yourselves therefore to God. Resist the devil, and he will flee from you. *Draw near to God, and he will draw near to you.* Cleanse your hands, you sinners, and purify your hearts, you double-minded.

> **2 Corinthians 4:6** For God, who said, "Let light shine out of darkness," has shone in our hearts to give the light of the knowledge of the glory of God in the face of Jesus Christ.

> **Matthew 5:13-16,**
> "*You are the salt of the earth*, but if salt has lost its taste, how shall its saltiness be restored? It is no longer good for anything except to be thrown out and trampled under people's feet. "*You are the light of the world.* A city set on a hill cannot be hidden. Nor do people light a lamp and put it under a basket, but on a stand, and it gives light

to all in the house. In the same way, *let your light shine before others*, so that they may see your good works and give glory to your Father who is in heaven.

Devotion is a discipline of starting the day with reading the Bible and communing with the Lord in prayer.

* It is a quiet time to focus on the Lord in prayer and reading of the Bible.
* It is a time set aside for spiritual communication with the Lord.
* It is a time spent in quiet conversation with the Lord.
* It is a time of self-examination.
* It is a time of confession and repentance.
* It is a time of asking forgiveness and also forgiving others.
* It is a time of personal reflection.

2 Timothy 2:15-16 (KJV) Study to shew thyself approved unto God, a workman that needeth not to be ashamed, rightly dividing the word of truth. But shun profane and vain babblings: for they will increase unto more ungodliness.

Daily devotions may be done early in the morning, afternoon, and/or at night. It is important that you set aside a quiet time that you would be able to focus on the Lord in prayer and Bible reading or studying on a regular basis. Devotion is a time when you are able to hear the voice of the Lord through Bible reading and studying. It is a time when you could use the Word of God to correct and purge yourself from sin and corruptible behavior.

Spending quality time in the presence of the Lord is a divine instruction that requires commitment and dedication. **Deuteronomy 11:19-28**,

You shall teach them to your children, talking of them when you are sitting in your house, and when you are walking by the way, and when you lie down, and when you rise. You shall write them on the doorposts of your house and on your gates, that your days and the days of your children may be multiplied in the land that the LORD swore to your fathers to give them, as long as the heavens are above the earth. For if you will be careful to do all this commandment that I command you to do, loving the LORD your God, walking in all his ways, and holding fast to him, then the LORD will drive out all these nations before you, and you will dispossess nations greater and mightier than you. Every place on which the sole of your foot treads shall be yours. Your territory shall be from the wilderness to the Lebanon and from the River, the river Euphrates, to the western sea. No one shall be able to stand against you. The LORD your God will lay the fear of you and the dread of you on all the land that you shall tread, as he promised you. "See, I am setting before you today a blessing and a curse: the blessing, if you obey the commandments of the LORD your God, which I command you today, and the curse, if you do not obey the commandments of the LORD your God, but turn aside from the way that I am commanding you today, to go after other gods that you have not known.

Orison

Orison is a prayer of plea. It is a fervent prayer asking for direction or guidance from the Lord. *Orison is a late Latin word (oratio) that means to speak to God. It is an old French word (orison) and Middle English (orisoun) which is considered archaic or no longer in use. (www.freedictionary.com)*

Earnest Hopes or Wishes

In the secular world, prayer is considered a wishful thought or earnest hope for an expectation of goodness upon a person or situation.

Intercession

Intercession is a prayer offered to God on behalf of another person or persons. (*See details in the following chapter*).

Intercession in Action

Prayer Focus
Need to understand spiritual communications

Goal
Need to know how to communicate with the Lord
Need to know how to make petitions that will attract the attention of Jehovah God
Need to know how to pronounce blessings according to divine order
Need my utterances to be effective before the throne of God

Prayer of Worship
O Lord God of heaven and earth,
You are the Great God of Wonders;
You are the all-knowing One,
The God of wisdom and knowledge;
O Lord, I worship and adore you,
Be thou exalted and uplifted in my life and endeavor.

Prayer of Confession and Repentance

O Lord, I confess the sins of my weaknesses and faults,
As I have made utterances that are not in line with your Word.
Because of lack of knowledge, I have offered ungodly prayers.
I have made pronouncements that are contrary to your
ordinances.
O Lord, I am sorry for making wrong utterances in
your presence.
O Lord, teach me how to make petitions and communi-
cate with you,
so that I will no longer repeat such errors in your presence.

Prayer of Forgiveness and Restoration

O Lord, forgive my weaknesses and ungodly utterances.
Wash and cleanse me with the blood that was shed for the
redemption of my soul.
Let the blood of Jesus redeem my mouth and utterances
from speaking unholy things.
O Lord, forgive and deliver me from wrong communications
in prayer.
O Lord, deliver and restore me with wisdom and knowledge,
To communicate with honor and respect to your throne.

Prayer of Petition

O Lord and my maker,
Please teach me how to pray, as the disciples requested in
Luke 11:1,
That I may know how to communicate with you, my Lord;
And that I may know how to make petitions that will attract
your attention;
O Lord, teach me to pronounce blessings according to your
divine order,
That my utterance may be effective and yield result
according to your plans and purposes in heaven.

Invocation of Blessings

O Lord God, the maker and restorer of our souls,
I hereby plead for the release of blessings upon my life.
O Lord, remember your Word and establish me in blessings,
according to Psalm 121:7-8 that says,
"The LORD shall preserve thee from all evil: he shall preserve thy soul.
The LORD shall preserve thy going out and thy coming in
from this time forth, and even for evermore."
O Lord, listen and hear my petition
whenever I lift up mine eyes unto the hills and cry for help.
O Lord, from you alone comes my help as you are the maker
of heaven and earth.
O Lord, bless and deliver me from evil,
for your Word declares that you will not suffer my foot
to be moved:
because "Behold, he that keepeth Israel [me] shall neither
slumber nor sleep.
The LORD is thy [my] keeper:
the LORD is thy [my] shade upon thy [my] right hand.
The sun shall not smite thee (me) by day, nor the moon by
night" (Ps. 121:4 KJV). Amen!

Song of Motivation:
Blessed Assurance

Blessed Assurance
Frances J. Crosby, pub. 1873
Copyright status is *Public Domain*
Subject: Assurance
Scripture: Hebrews 10:22

1. Blessed assurance, Jesus is mine!
   Oh, what a foretaste of glory divine!
   Heir of salvation, purchase of God,
   Born of His Spirit, washed in His blood.

   Refrain: This is my story, this is my song,
   Praising my Savior all the day long;
   This is my story, this is my song,
   Praising my Savior all the day long.

2. Perfect submission, perfect delight,
   Visions of rapture now burst on my sight;
   Angels, descending, bring from above
   Echoes of mercy, whispers of love.

3. Perfect submission, all is at rest,
   I in my Savior am happy and blest,
   Watching and waiting, looking above,
   Filled with His goodness, lost in His love.

Reference:
www.dictionary.reference.com
www.e-sword.com
www.freedictionary.com
www.library.timelesstruths.org/music/
Blessed Assurance Crosby/
www.Merriam-webster.com

www.mysticalblaze.com
www.Sacred-text.com/cla/tms08.htm
www.vocabulary.com

Chapter Three

The Realms of Intercessory Prayer

ntercessory prayer is simply referred to as intercession or prayer of intercession. Intercessory prayer is the act
of communication in which a person speaks to God on behalf
of another person or people. It is a humble plea requesting
God's intervention. It is a petition asking God's guidance and
leadership.

- The realm of intercessory prayer refers to the various
  types of pleas and agonizing prayers that are made
  at different times to gain the attention of the Most
  High God.
- It also refers to the technicalities of intercessory prayers,
  such as: the approaches, the intentions, the languages,
  and the expectations thereof.

This chapter will examine the various activities that take
place when one embarks on intercessory missions.

The Need for Intercession

The need for intercession calls for the need for intercessors,
priests, and prophets. Intercessors are not the same as warriors.

Intercessors cry to God for grace, mercy, and favor for divine interventions and encounters.

Warriors go to battlefields to fight against enemies, to set captives free, the open the prison gates, and pull down satanic strongholds.

Intercessory Warriors are those who have combined assignments to fight battles on their knees by crying aloud to God to take over their battles and send the angels of warfare on their behalf.

- **Independent Intercessors**: Independent intercessors are people who are all embracing in their responsibility to help and assist wherever there is a need. Irrespective of their relationship or affiliation, they pick up any burden that needs attention and start to carry it to the Lord for divine intervention.
- **Freelance Intercessors**: Independent intercessors can also be described as freelance intercessors because they are open to everyone and anyone who needs their professionalism in the realms of these affairs. They are ready to cry with those who cry and mourn with those who mourn. They are sensitive to people's needs and are very compassionate with matters that are related to humanity.
- Sometimes, both independent and freelance intercessors are able to connect with governmental authorities regarding matters that affect a people, an organization, or a nation.
- **Church Intercessors**: Church intercessors are the people or individuals that are appointed either directly or indirectly to support the ministers, congregation members, and some specific individuals within the church with prayer and fasting before the Lord. Sometimes, a church may appoint people to stand on behalf of the

denomination. Also, an individual or a group of people may feel led to carry and share in the burden of the minister or the leadership of a church as well as the burden of founder or pastor in charge.

- **Organizational Intercessors**: Some organizations have employees who are responsible for praying and asking the Lord for direction. The essence is to ensure that the will of the Lord is allowed to manifest so that the foundation on which that company is established may be honored and fulfilled without demonic influence.
- **Divine Intercessors**: Divine intercessors are those who are called directly and divinely assigned to carry the burden of the Lord. Such burdens may be over certain individuals, a people, an organization a nation, or even a governmental entity.

Divine intercessors go before the Lord on a regular basis to receive assignments to pray over. They are also sensitive to the nudging of the Holy Spirit at all times. The Lord may call upon them at any time to get on their needs, come into the intercessory room, or courtroom, to plead a case.

Therefore, all intercessors must have godly qualities to stand before our Father God. All intercessors and warriors must belong to a local church for protective covering. There is no independent soldier on the street. Independent warriors are sometimes classified as rebels who have no respect for legal or governmental authorities.

Also, an intercessor that does not belong to a local church and is not submissive to authority may easily become a prisoner of war or suffer unnecessary gunshots or assault from the enemy.

For that matter, the qualities of an intercessor include:

- Trustworthiness
- Submissiveness
- Obedience

- Humility
- Sensitivity
- Attentiveness
- Readiness

Intercession Demands Relationship

Relationship is an important factor in the realm of intercessory prayer. Without relationship, intercessory prayer would be difficult for both the intercessor and the petitioner or applicant.

In the realm of intercession, there are different parties playing different roles.

The Intercessor: First is the intercessor who may be a qualified priest, a prophet, or a minister of some sort, an individual or assigned person who is called to fulfill the responsibilities of standing in the gap for others.

- **The Priest**
- **The Prophet**

The Petitioner (Asker/Requestor): Second is the petitioner who is requesting the assistance of an intercessor to cry to the Lord on his/her behalf. The people of Israel asked Samuel to cry to God on their behalf.

> **1 Samuel 7:8-9** And the people of Israel said to Samuel, "Do not cease to cry out to the LORD our God for us, that he may save us from the hand of the Philistines." So Samuel took a nursing lamb and offered it as a whole burnt offering to the LORD. And Samuel cried out to the LORD for Israel, and the LORD answered him.

The relationship between an intercession and the Lord must be as such:

- It is important that the person acting as an intercessor who stands in the gap should have a personal relationship with Christ Jesus as Lord and Savior.
- The person acting as an intercessor on behalf of another or others must understand the importance of cleansing of the body, soul, and spirit by purification and sanctification.
- The person standing in the gap must understand the importance of holiness and righteousness of God.
- The intercessor must understand the role of grace and mercy with regards to the matter at stake.
- The intercessor must understand the legal grounds on which intercessory prayer operates.

Ezekiel 22:30 And I sought for a man among them who should build up the wall and stand in the breach before me for the land, that I should not destroy it, but I found none.

Isaiah 59:16 He saw that there was no *man, and wondered that there was no one to intercede*; then his own arm brought him salvation, and his righteousness upheld him.

Sacrificial Act

Standing in the gap to intercede on behalf of another person or people is a sacrificial offering. The person standing on behalf of others or an applicant must be aware of the demands required to perform the act of intercession.

A person responding to an intercessory mission must be ready to sacrifice his or her life to stand in the gap for both the known and unknown applicant that are making the request. The Lord Jesus used the term "my Father" in regard to God, and "my friends" in regard to believers to express the type and level of relationship as being very intimate.

John 15:13-17 Greater love has no one than this *that someone lay down his life for his friends.*

You are my friends if you do what I command you. No longer do I call you servants, for the servant does not know what his master is doing; *but I have called you friends, for all that I have heard from my Father I have made known to you.* You did not choose me, *but I chose you and appointed you that you should go and bear fruit and that your fruit should abide, so that whatever you ask the Father in my name, he may give it to you.* These things I command you, so that you will love one another.

Sacrifice of Love

Demonstration of love is a sacrificial act that fosters intercessory prayer. Persons who lack the ability to tolerate and endure other people because of their shortfalls or weaknesses may find it hard to stand in the gap of intercession. Even if they do go into intercession, instead of seeing the agony and suffering of Christ Jesus who redeemed us from sin, such persons would rather focus on the hurt and pain that hatred brings to them.

Once you take your eyes off the cross, all you see is your pain from failure, disappointment, rejection, hatred, and all the negative things that the world carries. Whereas, when you focus on the cross of Jesus, all you see is love as a result of the sacrifice for your redemption. His sacrifice is the reason for the blood that speaks on our behalf in time of intercession.

1 Peter 4:7-11,

The end of all things is at hand; therefore be self-controlled and sober-minded for the sake of your prayers. Above all, keep loving one another earnestly, since love covers a multitude of sins. Show hospitality to one another without grumbling. As each has received a gift, use it to serve one another, as good stewards of God's varied grace: whoever speaks, as one who speaks oracles of God; whoever serves, as one who serves by the strength that God supplies—in order that in everything God may be glorified through Jesus Christ. To him belong glory and dominion forever and ever. Amen.

Intercession Demands Intimacy

The petitioner must have an intimate relationship with the Lord. Christ Jesus is both the mediator and intercessor between God the Father and humankind. He stands in the court of heaven to appeal our case before the Lord as Satan the enemy brings accusation against us continuously.

Therefore, a person who desires to stand in the gap for others must seek to be like Jesus Christ who uses his own righteousness to protect us from the punishment of sinfulness and destruction.

John 17:11-12,

And I am no longer in the world, but they are in the world, and I am coming to you. Holy Father, keep them in your name, which you have given me, that they may be one, even as we are one. While I was with them, I kept them in your name, which you have given me. I have guarded them, and not one of them has been lost except the son of destruction, that the Scripture might be fulfilled.

A person whose heart is full of bitterness cannot stand in the gap to appeal for another or others. Also, a person who is selfish cannot be genuine enough to convince the Lord in a matter, since self-interest can easily prevail over other matters. Moses was not selfish, so he was able to remind the Almighty God concerning his promises to Abraham, Isaac and Jacob.

Exodus 32:10-14,

> Now therefore let me alone, that my wrath may burn hot against them and I may consume them, in order that I may make a great nation of you." But Moses implored the LORD his God and said, "O LORD, why does your wrath burn hot against your people, whom you have brought out of the land of Egypt with great power and with a mighty hand? Why should the Egyptians say, 'With evil intent did he bring them out, to kill them in the mountains and to consume them from the face of the earth'? Turn from your burning anger and relent from this disaster against your people. Remember Abraham, Isaac, and Israel, your servants, to whom you swore by your own self, and said to them, 'I will multiply your offspring as the stars of heaven, and all this land that I have promised I will give to your offspring, and they shall inherit it forever.'" And the LORD relented from the disaster that he had spoken of bringing on his people.

Intercession Demands Purity and Sanctification

God is holy; therefore, before one enters into his presence to make intercession, both the intercessor and the petitioner requesting assistance must reverence the Lord with purity of heart and sanctification. It is necessary for an intercessor to go through the process of cleansing and purification with genuineness all the time as it is necessary to take a bath and brush the mouth frequently. Lack of brushing the mouth frequently may cause the teeth to decay and also the mouth to have a bad smell. For instance, when one wakes up in the morning, one of the first things to do is to brush the mouth in order to avoid a bad odor from oozing out of the mouth. Lack of cleansing can cause one to suffer hindrance in the realms of the spirit, which may prevent one from gaining access into the presence of the Lord.

Cleansing is a spiritual method of releasing waste and impurity from the heart and mind. The things we see and hear can easily affect our mind and heart.

- The mind is the operating center where information is processed.
- The mind is the seat of the soul.
- The heart is the storage from where information is invested.
- The heart is the seat of the spirit.

Once information is stored in the heart, a person's character conforms to that information, and then it is exhibited in one's behavior.

Isaiah 63:5 I looked, but there was *no one to help; I was appalled, but there was no one to uphold;* so my own arm brought me salvation, and my wrath upheld me.

Psalm 106:23 Therefore he said he would destroy them—*had not Moses, his chosen one, stood in the breach before him*, to turn away his wrath from destroying them.

Intercession Demands Honesty and Sincerity

The person requesting prayer must be sincere and honest. If the truth of the matter is hidden, then prayer of lies and deception will be offered. Satan will step in to answer the prayers of deception because he is the Father of Lies.

Many people wonder why their prayers were not answered irrespective of many days of fasting. Well, any seed sown in deception will reap deception. It is important to sow what one expects to reap in harvest.

Psalm 18:25-26 With the merciful you show yourself merciful; with the blameless man you show yourself blameless; with the purified you show yourself pure; and with the crooked you make yourself seem tortuous.

Proverbs 12:17 Whoever speaks the truth gives honest evidence, but a false witness utters deceit.

Proverbs 24:26 Whoever gives an honest answer kisses the lips.

Luke 8:15 As for that in the good soil, they are those who, hearing the word, hold it fast in an honest and good heart, and bear fruit with patience.

Ephesians 4:28 Let the thief no longer steal, but rather let him labor, doing honest work with his own hands, so that he may have something to share with anyone in need.

The Price of Intercessory Warfare:

Daniel paid the price of faithfulness and integrity in order to secure a place in the realms of intercession. In the beginning, Daniel had sought for the Spirit of the Lord in order to operate in governmental spheres. As part of the qualities needed to influence governmental authorities, Daniel needed to possess and demonstrate unique abilities in the realms of dispensing knowledge, wisdom, and skillfulness. Anytime Daniel needed to perform his duties, his integrity came under attack. **Daniel 6:7, 12-24**,

All the high officials of the kingdom, the prefects and the satraps, the counselors and the governors are agreed that the king should establish an ordinance and enforce an injunction, *that whoever makes petition to any god or man for thirty days, except to you, O king, shall be cast into the den of lions ...*

Then they came near and said before the king, concerning the injunction, "O king! *Did you not sign an injunction, that anyone who makes petition to any god or man within thirty days except to you, O king, shall be cast into the den of lions?"* The king answered and said, "The thing stands fast, according to the law of the Medes and Persians, which cannot be revoked."

Then the king commanded, and *Daniel was brought and cast into the den of lions.* The king declared to Daniel, "May your God, whom you serve continually, deliver you!" *And a stone was brought and laid on the mouth of the den, and the king sealed it with his own signet and with the signet of his lords, that nothing might be changed concerning Daniel.* Then the king went to his palace and spent the night fasting; no diversions were brought to him, and sleep fled from him. Then, at break of day, the king arose and went in haste to the den of lions. As he came near to the den where Daniel was, *he cried out in a tone of anguish. The king declared to Daniel, "O Daniel, servant of the living God, has your God, whom you serve continually, been able to deliver you from the lions?"* Then Daniel said to the king, "O king, live forever! My God sent his angel and shut the lions' mouths, and they have not harmed me, because I was found blameless before him; and also before you, O king, I have done no harm." Then the king was exceedingly glad, and commanded that Daniel be taken up out of the den. *So Daniel was taken up out of the den, and no kind of harm was found on him, because he had trusted in his God.* And the king commanded, and those men who had maliciously accused Daniel were brought and cast into the den of lions—they, their children, and their wives. And before they reached the bottom of the den, the lions overpowered them and broke all their bones in pieces.

Intercession in Action

Prayer Focus
Request for Divine Intervention

Goal
Need for divine intervention in our lives and endeavors
Need for the Lord to hear our cry and intervene in all matters
presented before his throne
Need to know the difference between intercessory
and warring
So that we will rightly divide the word of truth
Need to know how to coordinate intercessory with warfare
Need to understand the burden of the Lord and per-
sonal burdens
Need to be sensitive to divine assignments and how to
perform it
in the realms of intercessory warfare

Prayer of Worship and Adoration
Dear Lord, our Father in heaven,
You deserve all the glory and honor;
Great and mighty are you in all the earth;
There is none like you.
Thank you, Lord, for your grace and mercy.
Thank you for your manifold blessings
Upon our lives.

Prayer of Confession and Repentance
O Lord, consider your grace and mercy,
As we confess and repent of all our wrongdoings,
That the sins of transgressions will not hinder us
from accessing your throne.
O Lord, we repent from any form of stubbornness,
That our behavior and attitude may not sever us from
your presence.

As your word declares in Proverbs 28:13 (KJV),
"He that covereth his sins shall not prosper:
but whoso confesseth and forsaketh them shall have mercy."
Therefore, we confess and renounce our sins,
That we may find mercy and gain favor in your sight, O Lord.

Prayer of Forgiveness and Restoration
O Lord, you are the merciful one that forgives,
Whenever we confess and repent of all unrighteousness.
O Lord, hear our cry and release us from the burden of sin,
According to Psalm 51:1-4,
"Have mercy upon me, O God, according to thy
lovingkindness:
according unto the multitude of thy tender mercies blot out
my transgressions.
Wash me throughly from mine iniquity, and cleanse me
from my sin.
For I acknowledge my transgressions: and my sin is ever
before me.
Against thee, thee only, have I sinned, and done this evil in
thy sight:
that thou mightest be justified when thou speakest,
and be clear when thou judgest."
O Lord, forgive and restore us unto yourself,
That we may be able to help the needy to come into
your presence.

Prayer of Petition
O Lord God of grace and mercy,
The One who hears and listens to the cry of the needy and
the helpless.
O Lord, hear our cry and intervene in all matters that con-
cerns our lives and endeavors.
O Lord, teach us to know the difference between intercessory
and warring,
So that we will rightly divide the word of truth;

Teach us to know how to coordinate intercessory with warfare prayers.,
So that we will understand the difference between the burden of the Lord
and personal desires.
O Lord, enable us to be sensitive to divine assignments,
and how to perform them in the realms of intercessory warfare,
So that your will be done on earth as it is in heaven;

Invocation of Blessings

O Lord, hear our petition and restore your blessings unto us;
According to Romans 15:13,
"Now the God of hope fill you with all joy and peace in believing,
that ye may abound in hope, through the power of the Holy Ghost."
O Lord, fill us with joy and peace in believing,
And cause us to abound in hope
Through the power of the Holy Spirit. Amen,

Song of Motivation
Teach Me Thy Way, O Lord

Teach Me Thy Way, O Lord
Words: Benjamin M. Ramsey, 1919.
Music: Camacha, Benjamin M. Ramsey

1. Teach me Thy way, O Lord,
   Teach me Thy way!
   Thy guiding grace afford,
   Teach me Thy way!
   Help me to walk aright,
   More by faith, less by sight;
   Lead me with heav'nly light,
   Teach me Thy way!

2. When I am sad at heart,
   Teach me Thy way!
   When earthly joys depart,
   Teach me Thy way!
   In hours of loneliness,
   In times of dire distress,
   In failure or success,
   Teach me Thy way!

3. When doubts and fears arise,
   Teach me Thy way!
   When storms o'erspread the skies,
   Teach me Thy way!
   Shine through the cloud and rain,
   Through sorrow, toil and pain;
   Make Thou my pathway plain,
   Teach me Thy way!

4. Long as my life shall last,
   Teach me Thy way!

Where'er my lot be cast,
Teach me Thy way!
Until the race is run,
Until the journey's done,
Until the crown is won,
Teach me Thy way!

Reference:
www.hymntime.com/tch/htm/t/e/

Chapter Four

The Technicalities of Intercessory Communications

The realm of intercessory prayer is like a courtroom procedure, where biblical laws are brought into fore. It is the sphere of considering the purpose of redemption and the position of Jesus Christ as the High Priest who presides as the spiritual attorney in the court of heaven.

Isaiah 28:10-13 (KJV),

> For precept must be upon precept, precept upon precept; line upon line, line upon line; here a little, and there a little: For with stammering lips and another tongue will he speak to this people. To whom he said, This is the rest wherewith ye may cause the weary to rest; and this is the refreshing: yet they would not hear. But *the word of the LORD was unto them precept upon precept, precept upon precept; line upon line, line upon line*; here a little, and there a little; that they might go, and fall backward, and be broken, and snared, and taken.

- **The Agenda**: Agenda has been described as a formal list of things to be done in a specific order. It usually consists of various matters that need to be dealt with in a meeting or gathering.

  An intercessor must approach the throne of God with specific matters to be presented for favor and mercy. The intercessor must also act like a scribe to take note of the list of things that the Lord may release as instruction and direction that needs to be followed.

- **The Approach**: As a type of prayer that focuses on pleading cases in the court of heaven, the attitude and methodology are sensitive. Intercessory prayer demands humility of character as one pleads for grace, mercy, favor, and compassion from the Most High God. Therefore, an intercessor must ensure that basic principles of cleansing and purity—spiritual protocol—are observed. (See my book for spiritual protocol: *Strategic Prayer Tactics I: Approach to Effective Communication*.)

- **The Intention**: The main purpose of intercessory prayer is to seek divine intervention for cases that are beyond human power and comprehension. Furthermore, it is to gain favor for grace and mercy before the Almighty God and mankind/governmental laws besides other matters.

- **The Language:** What differentiates a regular prayer from intercessory prayer is the language and tone of expression. Basically, intercessory prayer is a type of petition, so the language of warfare and confrontation must be carefully avoided or inculcated if/where necessary. Note that police officers are allowed to use their weapons in court to guard the environment from disgruntled elements, but they are not allowed to stir up civil unrest while expected to foster peace.

  Similarly, military officers are not allowed to carry their arms into a courthouse or use such weapons in a courtroom. The language of intercessory prayer is not the type that should stir up an uproar in the court of heaven. Although you may go to court to fight for your right and win victory, you must be careful not to use derogatory or defamatory language that is illegal before the law.

- For instance, although David was the king of Israel at the time that he committed adultery with Bathsheba, he humbled himself to observe spiritual protocol so that he could gain the favor of the Almighty God. In his prayer, he petitioned forgiveness by stating his offences as a result of his weaknesses thus:

Psalm 51:1-19,

To the choirmaster. A Psalm of David, when Nathan the prophet went to him, after he had gone in to Bathsheba.

Have mercy on me, O God,
according to your steadfast love;
according to your abundant mercy
blot out my transgressions.
Wash me thoroughly from my iniquity,
and cleanse me from my sin!
For I know my transgressions,
and my sin is ever before me.
Against you, you only, have I sinned
and done what is evil in your sight,
so that you may be justified in your words
and blameless in your judgment.
Behold, I was brought forth in iniquity,
and in sin did my mother conceive me.
Behold, you delight in truth in the inward being,
and you teach me wisdom in the secret heart.
Purge me with hyssop, and I shall be clean;
wash me, and I shall be whiter than snow.
Let me hear joy and gladness;

let the bones that you have broken rejoice.
Hide your face from my sins,
and blot out all my iniquities.
Create in me a clean heart, O God,
and renew a right spirit within me.
Cast me not away from your presence,
and take not your Holy Spirit from me.
Restore to me the joy of your salvation,
and uphold me with a willing spirit.
Then I will teach transgressors your ways,
and sinners will return to you.
Deliver me from bloodguiltiness,
O God, O God of my salvation,
and my tongue will sing aloud of your righteousness.
O Lord, open my lips,
and my mouth will declare your praise.
For you will not delight in sacrifice, or I would give it;
you will not be pleased with a burnt offering.
The sacrifices of God are a broken spirit;
a broken and contrite heart, O God, you will not despise.
Do good to Zion in your good pleasure; build up the
walls of Jerusalem;
then will you delight in right sacrifices,
in burnt offerings and whole burnt offerings;
then bulls will be offered on your altar.

- **The Expectation**: The purpose of intercessory prayer is
  to receive pardon, and be granted emancipation as Jesus
  gained victory on the cross of Calvary when he died to
  purchase our souls from the slavery of sin. Similarly,
  our expectation is to be granted favor and unusual intervention over whatever case we bring before the mercy
  throne of God.

One of the main purposes of spiritual communication is
to ask the Lord God for a change in an unfavorable situation.

Therefore, one goes into prayer with anticipation that the Lord will show forth his grace and mercy by responding with the power of intervention. "Now faith is the assurance of things hoped for, the conviction of things not seen." **(Hebrews 11:1)**

Studiousness

Studiousness is the act of learning and applying knowledge to the various aspects of life's endeavors as needed. Studiousness produces information that provides knowledge for the now and the morrow. Knowledge is power and wisdom is the security key that opens the door into the realms of intercession. To know what to say and how to say what is needed to be said is very important in the realms of intercession. Daniel was careful in the choice of his expression as he spoke the language of intercession to the king and leaders of Babylon, while he goes into the secret place of the Most High God to make spiritual appeals.

For instance, Daniel paid the price of knowledge, wisdom, and skillfulness in order to establish his divine call to the realms of intercession.

Daniel 1:5, 8-21,

The king assigned them a daily portion of the food that the king ate, and of the wine that he drank. *They were to be educated for three years, and at the end of that time they were to stand before the king.*

But Daniel resolved that he would not defile himself with the king's food, or with the wine that he drank. Therefore he asked the chief of the eunuchs to allow him not to defile himself. And *God gave Daniel favor and compassion* in the sight of the chief of the eunuchs, and the chief of the eunuchs said to Daniel, "I fear my lord the king, *who assigned your food and your drink*; for why should he see that you were in worse condition than the youths who are of your own age? So you would endanger my head with the king." Then Daniel said to the steward whom the chief of the eunuchs had assigned over Daniel, Hananiah, Mishael, and Azariah, *"Test your servants for ten days; let us be given vegetables to eat and water to drink. Then let our appearance and the appearance of the youths who eat the king's food be observed by you, and deal with your servants according to what you see." So he listened to them in this matter, and tested them for ten days.* At the end of ten days it was seen that they were better in appearance and fatter in flesh than all the youths who ate the king's food. So the steward took away their food and the wine they were to drink, and gave them vegetables.

As for these four youths, God gave them learning and skill in all literature and wisdom, and Daniel had understanding in all visions and dreams. At the end of the time, when the king had commanded that they should be brought in, the chief of the eunuchs brought them in before Nebuchadnezzar. And the king spoke with them, and *among all of them none was found like Daniel, Hananiah, Mishael, and Azariah. Therefore they stood before the king. And in every matter of wisdom and under-standing about which the king inquired of them, he found them ten times better than all the magicians and enchanters that were in all his kingdom. And Daniel was there until the first year of King Cyrus.*

Intercession in Action

Prayer Focus
Wisdom for Technicalities of Intercessory Communications

Goal
Need to understand the technicalities of intercessory prayer
Need wisdom of intercessory technicalities
Need wisdom for the application of intercessory
communications
Need to know how to set up intercessory agenda
Need to know how to approach the throne of grace and mercy
Need to speak the kind of language that corresponds with the
throne of mercy

Prayer of Worship and Adoration
O Lord God of heaven and earth,
You deserve the glory,
Honor and majesty belong to you;
You alone are Holy.

Prayer of Confession and Repentance
Lord, we honor your holiness as we confess and repent
from our sins of ignorance.
Lack of knowledge has caused us to make inappropriate
Pronouncements in your presence.
We have made unholy petitions and expected you to bless
our errors.
We have not considered your ordinances but have expected
you to prosper our compromises. O Lord, we are sorry for
allowing our ignorance and inabilities.
We shall no longer allow ignorance to rob us in our commu-
nications with you.

Prayer of Forgiveness and Restoration
O Lord, consider your grace and mercies,

Consider that you are the compassionate One who pardons
our iniquities;
O Lord, consider your word in Psalm 32:1-5 (KJV) that says,
*"Blessed is he whose transgression is forgiven, whose sin
is covered.*
*Blessed is the man unto whom the LORD imputeth
not iniquity,*
and in whose spirit there is no guile.
*When I kept silence, my bones waxed old through my roaring
all the day long.*
*For day and night thy hand was heavy upon me: my moisture
is turned into the drought of summer. Selah.*
*I acknowledged my sin unto thee, and mine iniquity have
I not hid. I said, I will confess my transgressions unto the
LORD; and thou forgavest the iniquity of my sin. Selah."*
O Lord, forgiveness is in your hand;
Therefore, consider your word and forgive us of all our
trespasses.
O Lord, release us from the burden of sin and restore us
unto yourself.

Prayer of Petition
O Lord God of mercy and compassion,
You are the living God that hears and listens to the cry of
your children,
For your word states in **Jeremiah 33:3,**
**"Call unto me, and I will answer thee, and shew thee great
and mighty things,
which thou knowest not."**
Therefore, I call upon you, O Lord God of mercy, be gra-
cious unto me,
And enable me to understand the technicalities of interces-
sory prayer.
O Lord, grant me wisdom of intercessory technicalities,
That I may present my petitions according to your precepts
and ordinances.

O Lord, grant me wisdom for the application of intercessory communications.
That my petitions will be made unto you—line upon line and precept upon precept,
According to your word in Isaiah 28:13 that says,
"But the word of the LORD was unto them precept upon precept, precept upon precept; line upon line, line upon line; here a little, and there a little ..."
O Lord, teach me how to set up intercessory agenda,
That I may know how to approach the throne of grace and mercy.
O Lord, enable me to speak the kind of language that corresponds with the throne of mercy;
Thank you, Lord, for hearing my cry and granting my petition.

Invocation of Blessings:
O Lord God of grace and mercy,
Consider your love and compassion,
And release your blessings unto us according to Romans 15:5-6 that says,
"Now the God of patience and consolation grant you to be likeminded one toward another according to Christ Jesus: That ye may with one mind and one mouth glorify God, even the Father of our Lord Jesus Christ."
Therefore, I declare the blessings of the technicalities of intercessory communications upon my life in Jesus's name.
I declare the word of the Lord and decree that, there shall be an ability to communicate with the Lord effectively in Jesus's name.
I declare the word of the Lord and decree that there shall be manifestation of blessings as we make petitions according to the ordinances of Jehovah God. Amen!

Song of Motivation
I Need Thee Every Hour

I Need Thee Every Hour
Annie S. Hawks, 1872
ref. by Robert Lowry, 1872
Copyright status is *Public Domain*
Subject: Supplication, Prayer
Scripture: Hebrews 4:16; I Thessalonians 5:17

1. I need Thee every hour, most gracious Lord;
   No tender voice like Thine can peace afford.

   Refrain:
   I need Thee, oh, I need Thee;
   Every hour I need Thee;
   Oh, bless me now, my Savior,
   I come to Thee.

3. I need Thee every hour, stay Thou nearby;
   Temptations lose their pow'r when Thou art nigh.

4. I need Thee every hour, in joy or pain;
   Come quickly and abide, or life is vain.

5. I need Thee every hour; teach me Thy will;
   And Thy rich promises in me fulfill.

6. I need Thee every hour, most Holy One;
   Oh, make me Thine indeed, Thou blessed Son.

Reference:
www.library.timelesstruths.org/
music/I_Need_Thee_Every_Hour/

Chapter Five

The Language And Dynamics Of Intercession

Intercessory Communication

Intercessory communications are not just prayers, but also various types of spiritual conversations and discussions as obtained in both the natural and the secular realms. Intercessory communication is a language that seeks to provide solution to all manner of situations—problems, challenges, and difficulties that confront humans in this life and beyond.

This chapter discusses the realms of intercessory prayer by examining the kind of language used to petition the Lord at different times and seasons.

Intercessory Connections: Intercessory communication is about connecting with the divine through contacting, consulting, interacting, exchanging, and transmitting information between mankind (an intercessor) and God.

Relationship: The power of effective communication demands some form of relationship such as friendship, acquaintance, association, link, or connection. Without a relationship, communication would be poor and unpleasant. Relationship makes communication easy and amicable. Therefore, the environment of intercessory prayer must be saturated with aromatic expressions that make communication responsive and effective. Therefore, it is essential to have a father-child relationship with the Lord in order to gain effective communication access to the Lord. Also, on a profession grounds, if you are called into the office of a priest or prophet, it is very important that you walk in a circumspective manner with the Lord in order to function effectively in the realms of intercession.

Contact: Contact is an essential need in the realms of intercessory prayer. Contact is a state in which communication is made possible. It is the grand access for connecting to the divine in order to share information, or to influence hope of petitioners crying unto the Lord for divine intervention. Also, it is the means of getting in touch by making a call to heaven, knocking on the gates of heaven, writing and/or presenting prayer requests, and speaking in the court of heaven.

- An intercessor must know how to contact the throne room of heaven.
- An intercessor must have access to the court of heaven.
- An intercessor must establish formidable contacts to provide access to information whenever necessary.

Exchange: Exchange is the act of sharing ideas or information between two or more persons by speaking or writing. It is also a system of using signs and symbols or behavior to communicate a message.

Exchange is a major aspect of communication in the realms of intercessory prayer. When we go into the presence of the Lord, we expect him to respond to our conversation and also discuss some matters as to why we have come into the chambers of his habitation. Three major things happen in the realms of exchange.

They are:

- **Access**: Ability to be connected to the throne room of heaven.
- **Message**: Ability to present a request and make petition in the manner that meets divine requirement.
- **Rapport**: Ability to have mutual conversation and discussion with understanding.

Consultation: Consultation is to ask for a specialist's or a professional's advice. One of the reasons for intercessory prayer is to seek the mind of God regarding a matter. Consultation is a place for gathering information and seeking the face of the Lord for direction. It is a place where the gifts of revelation operate effectively as the Lord speaks through visions, word knowledge, word of wisdom, and discernment.

The act of consultation includes the following:

- To ask for divine opinion
- To ask for divine permission
- To refer to the source of information, the Bible
- To check out information with regards to biblical promises
- To discuss a matter
- To seek divine advice
- To seek the perfect will of the Lord

Interaction: Interaction is a joint activity involving two or more people. It is a reciprocal action that has an effect on each other. It is the elementary force that put two people to work together.

A person desiring to fulfill the role of an intercessor must have a close and interactive relationship with the Lord. Interactive relationship involves the following:

- To interrelate
- To act together
- To network
- To intermingle

Transmission: Transmission is to spread a message by broadcasting. To transmit a message is to pass on information by putting it out in the air.

Language of Intercession

Language: Language is the means of communication that facilitates understanding to the hearer. Language expression can be verbally or nonverbally communicated.

Verbal language is a communication system where people use spoken or written words to express their thoughts, intensions, and actions.

Nonverbal language is the use of signs and gestures or inarticulate sounds to communicate something. There are different types of expression of tongues that represent a variety of languages among different groups of people that dwell together in a particular sphere of activities. Such a natural way of expression can be described as the native language of a people in a particular environment—in cities, towns, and nations. Various expressions of tongues can be broken down into dialect, patois, vernacular, idiom, jargon, argot, slang, and such like.

Another form of language expression can be categorized as words, prose, poetry, phrase, verbal skills, and style.

Utterance: Utterance is the expression of word made by making a vocal sound, a speech, a statement, a remark, or declaration.

Dynamics of Intercessory Language

Dynamics of intercessory language has to do with the kind of expression that is expected during intercessory communication. In a place of learning, there is supposed to be an open forum for interaction. One of the aims of interaction is to allow questions to be asked in order to derive understanding or solution to a problem without assumption.

The language of intercessory prayer involves different types of communicative expressions that include such as:

- Asking
- Seeking
- Knocking
- Attention
- Listening
- Hearing
- Expectation

The dynamics of intercessory language is derived from the command that the Lord Jesus gave in **Matthew 7:7-10**,

> *Ask, and it will be given to you; seek, and you will find; knock, and it will be opened to you.* For everyone who asks receives, and the one who seeks finds, and to the one who knocks it will be opened. Or which one of you, if his son asks him for bread, will give him a stone? Or if he asks for a fish, will give him a serpent? If you then, who are evil, know how to give good gifts to your children, how much more will your Father who is in heaven give good things to those who ask him!

Asking

The Realms of Asking: In the realms of intercessory prayer, asking a question is very appropriate. In some cultural settings and traditions, there is an assumption that asking a question is a sign of disrespect for the elderly and people in authority. This kind of assumption affects how people view the matter of asking questions during prayer.

Some people find it offensive and disrespectful when they are asked questions. Some people also have a habit of not answering questions. While some people use questions to oppose questions being asked instead of providing an answer to the question asked.

For instance, when you try to greet or share pleasantries with some people by asking, "How are you?" They return the same question to you, "How are you" instead of responding, "I'm fine/good. Thank you." I heard a lady once said, "You are too young to ask how I'm doing, okay!" With that kind of mentality, it will be a difficult thing to express oneself in prayer.

In one of the models of the various prayers that Christ Jesus taught, he provided us with room to have interaction with our heavenly Father.

Christ Jesus stated in **Matthew 7:7-8**,

> "Ask, and it will be given to you; seek, and you
> will find; knock, and it will be opened to you.
> For everyone who asks receives, and the one
> who seeks finds, and to the one who knocks it
> will be opened.

All manner of requests are taking place in the realm of intercession as in general prayers. Sometimes, the cause of intercession is to make a request for a divine intervention, while some requests are demanding divine encounters and arrests.

The System of Asking: In the realm of intercession, asking is a system of obtaining an answer or some form of information.

- It is a type of expression that enables you to gain access to something.
- It is to pose a question in order to get an answer.

Asking is a type of interrogation, query, and inquiry that addresses a person in order to gain information.

- **To Inquire**: is to find out the truth about something. It is also to find out what to do and how to do.
- **To Request**: is to petition, plead for favor and mercy.
- **To Interrogate**: is a systematic order of questioning in to obtain details, especially in court or by a prosecutor.
- **To Query**: is an authoritative manner of obtaining information without injecting an iota of familiarity.
- **To Demand:** is a system of making a forceful request in a manner that is difficult to ignore.

  ➢ It is to command, put pressure or stress for a desire to be met.
  ➢ It is an urgent requirement for resources or action.
  ➢ It is a legal action for compliance.

- **To Solicit**: is a means of announcing one's wants or needs by attracting public attention. It is to advertise one's desires to the public.
- **Expect**: is to wait patiently for an answer in anticipation that your petition has been heard as presented.

Asking in Prayer

Asking in prayer is based on relationship. There are about 3,300 questions in the Bible, although all questions were not identified with the required punctuation.

There are various reasons why people may need to ask questions while in the presence of the Lord. In the realms of their divine encounters with the angel of the Lord, both Zachariah and the Virgin Mary asked questions to which they received answers.

Zechariah Asked a Question: Zechariah asked the angel of the Lord a question when he was visited in the temple. Although Zechariah doubted the details of the message, the angel still answered his question.

Luke 1:5-20,

> In the days of Herod, king of Judea, there was a priest named Zechariah, of the division of Abijah. And he had a wife from the daughters of Aaron, and her name was Elizabeth. And they were both righteous before God, walking blamelessly in all the commandments and statutes of the Lord. But they had no child, because Elizabeth was barren, and both were advanced in years. *Now while he was serving as priest before God when his division was on duty, according to the custom of the priesthood, he was chosen by lot to enter the temple of the Lord and burn incense.* And the whole multitude of the *people were praying outside at the hour of incense.* And there appeared to him *an angel of the Lord standing on the right side of the altar of incense.* And Zechariah was troubled when he saw him, and fear fell upon him. But the angel said to him, *"Do not be afraid, Zechariah, for your prayer has been heard, and your wife Elizabeth will bear you a son, and you shall call his name John. And you will have joy and gladness, and many will rejoice at his birth, for*

he will be great before the Lord. And he must not drink wine or strong drink, and he will be filled with the Holy Spirit, even from his mother's womb. And he will turn many of the children of Israel to the Lord their God, and he will go before him in the spirit and power of Elijah, to turn the hearts of the fathers to the children, and the disobedient to the wisdom of the just, to make ready for the Lord a people prepared." And Zechariah said to the angel, *"How shall I know this? For I am an old man, and my wife is advanced in years."* And the angel answered him, *"I am Gabriel. I stand in the presence of God, and I was sent to speak to you and to bring you this good news. And behold, you will be silent and unable to speak until the day that these things take place,* because you did not believe my words, which will be fulfilled in their time."

Mary Asked a Question: The Virgin Mary questioned the angel of the Lord when she received a divine encounter, which gave her detailed explanation of what the Lord intended to do with her.

Luke 1:28-38,

And he came to her and said, "Greetings, O favored one, the Lord is with you!" But she was greatly troubled at the saying, and tried to discern what sort of greeting this might be. And *the angel said to her*, "Do not be afraid, Mary, for you have found favor with God. And behold, you will conceive in your womb and bear a son, and you shall call his name Jesus. He will be great and will be called the Son of the Most High. And the Lord God will give to him the throne of his father David, and he will reign over the house of Jacob forever, and of his kingdom there will be no end."

And Mary said to the angel, "How will this be, since I am a virgin?"

And the angel answered her, "The Holy Spirit will come upon you, and the power of the Most High will overshadow you; therefore the child to be born will be called holy—the Son of God. And behold, your relative Elizabeth in her old age has also conceived a son, and this is the sixth month with her who was called barren. For nothing will be impossible with God." And Mary said, "Behold, I am the servant of the Lord; let it be to me according to your word." And the angel departed from her.

Some questions were posed to Paul out of a burden requesting help. As in **Acts 16:30-31**, "Then he brought them out and said, 'Sirs, what must I do to be saved?' And they said, 'Believe in the Lord Jesus, and you will be saved, you and your household.'"

Nicodemus's Question: During a conversation between the Lord and one of the rulers of the Jews, a man called Nicodemus asked him an interesting spiritual question that has become the basis for our relationship with Christ Jesus: **John 3:4-7,**

Nicodemus said to him, *"How can a man be born when he is old? Can he enter a second time into his mother's womb and be born?"* Jesus answered, "Truly, truly, I say to you, unless one is born of water and the Spirit, he cannot enter the kingdom of God. That which is born of the flesh is flesh, and that which is born of the Spirit is spirit. Do not marvel that I said to you, *'You must be born again.'"*

Asking in prayer is based on relationship. As the Lord Jesus explained to Nicodemus, unless one has experienced the spiritual birth, one cannot claim to have a personal relationship with the Lord. **Matthew 7:8-11,**

For everyone who asks receives, and the one who seeks finds, and to the one who knocks it will be opened. Or which one of you, if his son asks him for bread, will give him a stone? Or if he asks for a fish, will give him a serpent? If you then, who are evil, know how to give good gifts to your children, how much more will your Father who is in heaven give good things to those who ask him!

According to His Will: Knowing the will of the Lord is very vital in prayer communication. He gives the assurance that if our request is based on his will, he will surely answer. That means there is need to consider the will of God before we make petitions to him. **First John 5:14-15** says, "And this is the confidence that we have toward him, that if we ask anything according to his will he hears us. And if we know that he hears us in whatever we ask, we know that we have the requests that we have asked of him."

Ask in his name: When should you ask, and what are you supposed to ask?

- Ask according to the will of God.

- Ask in his name.
- Ask and it shall be given unto you.

John 14:14-18

> If you *ask me anything in my name, I will do it.*
> "If you love me, you will *keep my command-*
> *ments.* And I will *ask the Father,* and he will
> give you another Helper, to be with you forever,
> even the Spirit of truth, whom the world cannot
> receive, because it neither sees him nor *knows*
> *him. You know him, for he dwells with you and*
> *will be in you. "I will not leave you as orphans;*
> *I will come to you.*

Ask and He Will Answer

Jeremiah 33:2-3

> "Thus says the LORD who made the earth, the
> LORD who formed it to establish it—the LORD
> is his name: *Call to me and I will answer you,*
> *and will tell you great and hidden things that*
> *you have not known.*

The Secret Things: What are the secret things that could only
be revealed through intercessory prayer? **Deuteronomy 29:29**
says, "The secret things belong to the LORD our God, but the
things that are revealed belong to us and to our children forever,
that we may do all the words of this law."

The Lord has shown new and hidden things.

Isaiah 48:6-7

> You have heard; now see all this;
> and will you not declare it?
> From this time forth I announce to you
> new things,
> hidden things that you have not known. They
> are created now, not long ago;
> before today you have never heard of them,
> lest you should say, "Behold, I knew them."

The Lord provides an assurance when one asks by calling upon him for help.

> **Psalm 91:15-16** says, "When he calls to me, I
> will answer him; I will be with him in trouble;
> I will rescue him and honor him. With long life
> I will satisfy him and show him my salvation."

God is ready to answer when we call.

> **Isaiah 65:24** Before they call I will answer;
> while they are yet speaking I will hear.

> **Matthew 21:21-22** And Jesus answered them,
> "Truly, I say to you, if you have faith and do not
> doubt, you will not only do what has been done
> to the fig tree, but even if you say to this moun-
> tain, 'Be taken up and thrown into the sea,' it
> will happen. And *whatever you ask in prayer*,
> you will receive, if you have faith."

> **Mark 11:24-25** Therefore I tell you, *what-
> ever you ask in prayer, believe that you have
> received it, and it will be yours.* And whenever
> you stand praying, forgive, if you have anything

against anyone, so that your Father also who is in heaven may forgive you your trespasses."

John 14:13-14 *Whatever you ask in my name, this* I will do, that the Father may be glorified in the Son. *If you ask me anything in my name, I will do it.*

John 15:7 If you abide in me, and my words abide in you, *ask whatever you wish, and it will be done for you.*

1 John 3:21-22 Beloved, if our heart does not condemn us, we have confidence before God; and *whatever we ask we receive from him,* because we keep his commandments and do what pleases him.

1 John 5:14 And this is the confidence that we have toward him, that *if we ask anything according to his will he hears us.*

Seeking

The Realm of Seeking: Seeking is one of the major characteristics of intercessory prayer. It is an earnest effort to accomplish solution in the realms of prayer. It is a conscientious activity to achieve a purpose.

- Seeking is to search for the will of the Lord concerning a matter. It requires some technicalities that include consecration. The priest or intercessor is required to observe some level of purity in order to be able to perform their duty.

1 Chronicles 15:12-15,

> And [David] said to them, "You are the heads of the fathers' houses of the Levites. *Consecrate yourselves, you and your brothers, so that you may bring up the ark of the LORD*, the God of Israel, to the place that I have prepared for it. Because you did not carry it the first time, the LORD our God broke out against us, *because we did not seek him according to the rule*." So the priests and the Levites consecrated themselves to bring up the ark of the LORD, the God of Israel. And the Levites carried the ark of God on their shoulders with the poles, as Moses had commanded according to the word of the LORD.

Christ Jesus commanded us to "*seek first the kingdom of God and his righteousness, and all these things will be added to you*." (**Matthew 6:33**)

- It is a cry and plea to God to show you your destiny.
- It is a cry and plea for the manifestation of scriptural word of the Lord.
- It is a cry and plea for divine instruction and direction to manage your life endeavors.
- It is a cry and plea for divine intervention and encounter.
- It is a cry and plea for achievement and fulfillment.
- It is a cry and plea for solutions.
- It is a cry and plea for grace and mercy.
- It is a cry and plea for uncommon favor.
- It is a cry and plea for justice.
- It is a cry and plea for restoration.

Seeking is an earnest and conscientious activity intended to do or accomplish something.

- Attempt to find a solution
- Try to discover and recover
- Seek permission
- Seek approval
- Seek refuge

When, What, and How to Seek

In time of war: David sought the Lord when he was plundered by the enemy. He inquired if he should pursue the enemy involved. The Lord encouraged him to pursue, overtake, and possess all that had been stolen from him.

1 Samuel 30:8-9,

> And *David inquired of the LORD, "Shall I pursue after this band? Shall I overtake them?"* He answered him, *"Pursue, for you shall surely overtake and shall surely rescue."* So David set out, and the six hundred men who were with him, and they came to the brook Besor, where those who were left behind stayed.

Persistent Prayer on Legal Grounds: Seeking is a type of persistent prayer whereby the petitioner does not give up, but continues to cry and plead her course until her unmet need is met. Christ Jesus gave a parable of a widow who did not stop crying until an earthly king gave her what she requested. However, that needs was justified based on legal grounds. So the Lord refers to that need as justice. **Luke 18:1-8,**

> And he told them a parable to the effect that they ought *always to pray and not lose heart.* He said, "In a certain city there was a judge who neither feared God nor respected man. And there was a widow in that city who kept coming to him and

saying, 'Give me justice against my adversary.'
For a while he refused, but afterward he said to
himself, 'Though I neither fear God nor respect
man, yet *because this widow keeps bothering
me, I will give her justice*, so that she will not
beat me down by her continual coming.'" And
the Lord said, "Hear what the unrighteous judge
says. And *will not God give justice to his elect,
who cry to him day and night? Will he delay
long over them?* I tell you, *he will give justice
to them speedily*. Nevertheless, when the Son of
Man comes, will he find faith on earth?"

Seeking must be done based on the perfect will of God.
Romans 12:1-2,

I appeal to you therefore, brothers, *by the mercies of God,* to present your bodies as a living
sacrifice, holy and acceptable to God, which is
your spiritual worship. Do not be conformed to
this world, but be transformed by the renewal of
your mind, that by testing you may discern *what
is the will of God, what is good and acceptable
and perfect*.

Selfish and Vain Prayers: Sometimes people are entrenched
in fasting and praying over matters that are illegal and expect
the Lord to grant their heart desires. Illegal prayers are desires
that are ungodly and unbiblical, as they are only meant to satisfy self without fulfilling the glory of the Lord. A petition is
selfish when one indulges in envy and lust for what belongs to
another person, yet fasting and praying to dispossess the owner
of his or her worth.

James 4:3 You ask and do not receive, because
you ask wrongly, to spend it on your passions.

James 1:6 But let him ask in faith, with no doubting, for the one who doubts is like a wave of the sea that is driven and tossed by the wind.

1 Chronicles 22:19 Now set your mind and heart to seek the LORD your God. Arise and build the sanctuary of the LORD God, so that the ark of the covenant of the LORD and the holy vessels of God may be brought into a house built for the name of the LORD."

Colossians 3:1-2 If then you have been raised with Christ, *seek the things that are above, where Christ is, seated at the right hand of God. Set your minds on things that are above, not on things that are on earth.*

Psalm 105:4 Seek the LORD and his strength; seek his presence continually!

The Face of the Lord: Seeking the face of the Lord means seeking the glory and brightness of his personal character. An intercessor must set his or her heart and mind on God and his purpose.

Matthew 28:20 "Teaching them to observe all that I have commanded you. And behold, I am with you always, to the end of the age."

2 Thessalonians 3:5 *May the Lord direct your hearts* to the love of God and to the steadfastness of Christ.

Job 8:5-6 If you will *seek God and plead with the Almighty for mercy, if you are pure and upright,* surely then he will rouse himself for you and restore your rightful habitation.

Psalm 34:4 *I sought the LORD, and he answered me* and delivered me from all my fears.

Psalm 37:4 *Delight yourself in the LORD,* and he will give you the desires of your heart.

Isaiah 30:19 For a people shall dwell in Zion, in Jerusalem; you shall weep no more. *He will surely be gracious to you at the sound of your cry.* As soon as he hears it, he answers you.

Jeremiah 29:12-14

> *Then you will call upon me and come and pray to me, and I will hear you. You will seek me and find me,* when you seek me with all your heart. *I will be found by you, declares the LORD,* and I will restore your fortunes and gather you from all the nations and all the places where I have driven you, declares the LORD, and I will bring you back to the place from which I sent you into exile.

Pride is a Hindrance: Pride is one of the hindrances to seeking the Lord.

> **Psalm 10:4** In the pride of his face the wicked does not seek him; all his thoughts are, "There is no God."

The Benefit of Seeking the Lord: The Lord rewards those who seek him diligently with fear and trembling. An intercessor must seek the Lord diligently without a hidden agenda to covet what belongs to other persons. The prayer of covetousness is dangerous, as the Ten Commandment also warned against the sin.

First Chronicles 28:9-10

> And you, Solomon my son, know the God of your father and serve him with a whole heart and with a willing mind, for the LORD searches all hearts and understands every plan and thought. *If you seek him, he will be found by you, but if you forsake him, he will cast you off forever.* Be careful now, for the LORD has chosen you to build a house for the sanctuary; be strong and do it.

> **Hebrews 11:6** And without faith it is impossible to please him, for whoever would draw near to God must believe that he exists and that *he rewards those who seek him.*

Knocking

The System of Knocking: Knocking is a deep level of intercession where there is a high level of groaning and wailing before the Lord. It is a high intensity of prayer, where words cannot express the depth of the agony of pain and suffering that one might be experiencing. It is an act of reminding the Lord to remember his promises and pour out his blessings upon his people on earth.

Knocking is the legal grounds that give us the authority to present our case before the Lord with groaning and crying until the Lord releases mercy and justice unto us.

During the days of Esther, when Haman decided to annihilate the Jewish race living in the kingdom of Persia, the Jews cried and wailed unto the Lord for deliverance. Their legal access to the Lord was the act of fasting which they employed with helplessness.

The Realm of Knocking

Knocking can be described as wailing, groaning, and lamenting. Scripture states that the Holy Spirit groans for us while interceding on our behalf. **Romans 8:26-28**,

> Likewise the Spirit helps us in our weakness. For we do not know what to pray for as we ought, *but the Spirit himself intercedes for us with groanings too deep for words.* And he who searches hearts knows what is the mind of the Spirit, because *the Spirit intercedes for the saints according to the will of God.* And we know that for those who love God all things work together for good, *for those who are called according to his purpose.*

Wailing: It is to make a mournful cry to express pain, grief, and misery. It can be described as moaning, weeping, crying, and screaming.

Lamenting: is an expression of grief whereby one cries out of pain.

Groaning: Growling, sighing, wailing, and lamenting are unique ways of knocking the doors of heaven and drumming oneself into the presence of the King of Glory.

Through wailing and lamenting, the Jewish people gained access to the throne room of God in heaven—the kingdom of God, which granted favor and access to Esther before the Persian king on earth—the kingdom of man.

Knocking is an act of blowing the trumpet of the Lord.

- It is an act of storming the gates of heaven with an SOS cry for help.
- It is a deliberate noise made to attract attention.
- It is a repetitive noise.

When, Where, and How to Knock.

How to Knock

1. Identify the Problem: In order to go into intercessory petition, you need to identify the problem or the case which is demanding a petition or an appeal. An intercessor must not go to court without understanding the case for petitioning. The problem here is that Haman had secured a decree with the king's signet to annihilate the Jews. **Esther 3:8, 13-15**,

> Then Haman said to King Ahasuerus, *"There is a certain people scattered abroad and dispersed among the peoples in all the provinces of your kingdom. Their laws are different from those of every other people, and they do not keep the king's laws, so that it is not to the king's profit to tolerate them. …*
>
> Letters were sent by couriers to all the king's provinces with *instruction to destroy, to kill, and to annihilate all Jews, young and old, women and children, in one day*, the thirteenth day of the twelfth month, which is the month of Adar, and to plunder their goods. A copy of the document was to be issued as a decree in every

province by proclamation to all the peoples to be ready for that day. The couriers went out hurriedly by order of the king, and the decree was issued in Susa the citadel. And *the king and Haman sat down to drink, but the city of Susa was thrown into confusion.*

2. Cry Out for Help: No matter who you are, learn to cry out for help when the enemy tries to attack and destroy your people. Notify them concerning the matter and gather yourselves together for support and encouragement. Demonstrate an act of unity and lift up one voice before the Lord to seek help as you knock on the doors of authority for divine intervention.

Esther 4:1-3, 7-17,

> When Mordecai learned all that had been done, *Mordecai tore his clothes and put on sackcloth and ashes, and went out into the midst of the city, and he cried out with a loud and bitter cry.* He went up to the entrance of the king's gate, for *no one was allowed to enter the king's gate clothed in sackcloth.* And in every province, wherever the king's command and his decree reached, *there was great mourning among the Jews, with fasting and weeping and lamenting, and many of them lay in sackcloth and ashes. ...* and Mordecai told him all that had happened to him, *and the exact sum of money that Haman had promised to pay into the king's treasuries for the destruction of the Jews. Mordecai also gave him a copy of the written decree issued in Susa for their destruction, that he might show it to Esther and explain it to her and command her to go to the king to beg his favor and plead with him on behalf of her people.* And Hathach went

and told Esther what Mordecai had said. Then Esther spoke to Hathach and commanded him to go to Mordecai and say, "All the king's servants and the people of the king's provinces know that *if any man or woman goes to the king inside the inner court without being called, there is but one law—to be put to death, except the one to whom the king holds out the golden scepter so that he may live.* But as for me, I have not been called to come in to the king these thirty days." And they told Mordecai what Esther had said. Then Mordecai told them to reply to Esther, *"Do not think to yourself that in the king's palace you will escape any more than all the other Jews. For if you keep silent at this time, relief and deliverance will rise for the Jews from another place,* but you and your father's house will perish. And *who knows whether you have not come to the kingdom for such a time as this?"* Then Esther told them to reply to Mordecai, *"Go, gather all the Jews to be found in Susa, and hold a fast on my behalf, and do not eat or drink for three days, night or day. I and my young women will also fast as you do. Then I will go to the king, though it is against the law, and if I perish, I perish."* Mordecai then went away and *did everything as Esther had ordered him.*

3. File Your Case in Court on Legal Grounds: For you to gain a hearing in the court of law, you must file your case on legal grounds. Thus the high priest or intercessor must ensure that you have a legal right to file your case. In other words, you are walking and living in obedience to the commands of the Lord. You have not misbehaved or defiled yourself in the matter of concern. You have not transgressed the statutes of the Most

High God. You are righteous and just before the Lord. Your request is not based on selfishness and vanity.

Esther gathered momentum based on the advice of her uncle Mordecai and decided to file her case in the court of heaven and on earth. The three days' fast that followed the initial crying and moaning of the Jews throughout the Persian kingdom had open the doors of wisdom and favor from the throne room of Jehovah God. It was time to file the petition before the earthly king.

At this point, Esther took the risk and bold step to access the throne of King Ahasuerus as she believed that the fasting and groaning of her people had granted her favor before the king. And of course, the king's response toward Esther was positive and favorable. **Esther 5:1-5,**

> On the third day *Esther put on her royal robes* and stood in the inner court of the king's palace, in front of the king's quarters, *while the king was sitting on his royal throne inside the throne room* opposite the entrance to the palace. And *when the king saw Queen Esther standing in the court, she won favor in his sight,* and he held out to Esther the golden scepter that was in his hand. Then Esther approached and touched the tip of the scepter. And *the king said to her, "What is it, Queen Esther? What is your request? It shall be given you, even to the half of my kingdom."* And Esther said, "If it please the king, let the king and Haman come today to a feast that I have prepared for the king." Then the king said, *"Bring Haman quickly, so that we may do as Esther has asked."* So the king and Haman came to the feast that Esther had prepared.

4. Expect Divine Favor and Intervention: When you walk with the Lord in the light of his Word and do not transgress his law, he will fight a series of battles concerning your whole life. Scripture states that obedience is better than sacrifice.

Esther and her people did not know how the Lord would fight their battles against Haman, yet they were in anticipation of a glorious victory. For the Lord had given them a series of promises to protect and deliver them from evil.

a. One of the first things that happened after the fast was that Esther gained tremendous favor before the king and Haman the destroyer, so that Esther was welcomed into the court and presence of the king.
b. The second, the king gave Esther a red carpet to request anything that she desired up to half of his kingdom. And whatever Esther asked for was granted her without condition. On two occasions, the king asked Esther for her wish and request.

Esther 7:2 And on the second day, as they were drinking wine after the feast, the king again said to Esther, *"What is your wish, Queen Esther? It shall be granted you. And what is your request? Even to the half of my kingdom, it shall be fulfilled."*

c. **The third** is that the king agreed to attend Esther's banquet with Haman as requested.
d. **The fourth** was that Mordecai, the uncle of Esther, was promoted by the very Haman, who was the enemy who had planned to destroy him and his people, the Jews.

Esther 6:6-13,

> So Haman came in, and the king said to him, "What should be done to the man whom the king delights to honor?" And Haman said to himself, "Whom would the king delight to honor more than me?" And Haman said to the king, "For the man whom the king delights to honor,

let royal robes be brought, which the king has worn, and the horse that the king has ridden, and on whose head a royal crown is set. And let the robes and the horse be handed over to one of the king's most noble officials. Let them dress the man whom the king delights to honor, and let them lead him on the horse through the square of the city, proclaiming before him: 'Thus shall it be done to the man whom the king delights to honor.'" *Then the king said to Haman, "Hurry; take the robes and the horse, as you have said, and do so to Mordecai the Jew, who sits at the king's gate. Leave out nothing that you have mentioned."* So Haman took the robes and the horse, and he dressed Mordecai and led him through the square of the city, proclaiming before him, *"Thus shall it be done to the man whom the king delights to honor."* Then Mordecai returned to the king's gate. But Haman hurried to his house, mourning and with his head covered. And Haman told his wife Zeresh and all his friends everything that had happened to him. Then his wise men and his wife Zeresh said to him, *"If Mordecai, before whom you have begun to fall, is of the Jewish people, you will not overcome him but will surely fall before him."*

e. **The fifth** is that Esther did not rush her petition but allowed wisdom and patience to lead her through carefully so that she would not mess up her appeal to deliver the Jews. Esther ensured that she was secured in the king's favor before she exposed the enmity perpetrated in Haman.

➤ For her wish, Esther petitioned for her personal life to be spared.
➤ For her request, she petitioned for her people not to be destroyed.

Esther 7:1-6,

So the king and Haman went in to feast with Queen Esther. And on the second day, as they were drinking wine after the feast, the king again said to Esther, *"What is your wish, Queen Esther? It shall be granted you. And what is your request? Even to the half of my kingdom, it shall be fulfilled."* Then Queen Esther answered, *"If I have found favor in your sight, O king, and if it please the king, let my life be granted me for my wish, and my people for my request. For we have been sold, I and my people, to be destroyed, to be killed, and to be annihilated.* If we had been sold merely as slaves, men and women, I would have been silent, for our affliction is not to be compared with the loss to the king." Then King Ahasuerus said to Queen Esther, *"Who is he, and where is he, who has dared to do this?"* And Esther said, *"A foe and enemy! This wicked Haman!"* Then Haman was terrified before the king and the queen.

The Lord fought a series of battles for Esther and her people more than they ever requested. Every evil plan and decree that Haman had purported for Mordecai and the Jews went into reverse. The crying and groaning of the Jews that was supported with fasting sent a knock on the doors of heaven. **Esther 7:7-10,**

And the king arose in his wrath from the wine-drinking and went into the palace garden, but Haman stayed to beg for his life from Queen Esther, for he saw that harm was determined against him by the king. And the king returned from the palace garden to the place where they were drinking wine, as Haman was falling on the couch where Esther was. And the king said, *"Will he even assault the queen in my presence, in my own house?"* As the word left the mouth of the king, they covered Haman's face. Then Harbona, one of the eunuchs in attendance on the king, said, "Moreover, the gallows that Haman has prepared for Mordecai, whose word saved the king, is standing at Haman's house, fifty cubits high." And the king said, *"Hang him on that." So they hanged Haman on the gallows that he had prepared for Mordecai. Then the wrath of the king abated.*

f. **The sixth** is a new level of promotion opened up for Mordecai. Haman's position was taken over by Mordecai. **Esther 8:1-2**,

On that day King Ahasuerus gave to Queen Esther the house of Haman, the enemy of the Jews. And Mordecai came before the king, for Esther had told what he was to her. And the king took off his signet ring, which he had taken from Haman, and gave it to Mordecai. And Esther set Mordecai over the house of Haman.

g. **The seventh** was that Esther entreated the king to reverse the evil plan that Haman had plotted against the Jews. After Haman had been eliminated from the scene, Esther entered another level of appeal to revoke the decree that Haman had plotted against her people. **Esther 8:3-7**,

Then Esther spoke again to the king. *She fell at his feet and wept and pleaded with him to avert the evil plan of Haman the Agagite and the plot that he had devised against the Jews.* When the king held out the golden scepter to Esther, Esther rose and stood before the king. And she said, *"If it please the king, and if I have found favor in his sight, and if the thing seems right before the king, and I am pleasing in his eyes, let an order be written to revoke the letters devised by Haman the Agagite, the son of Hammedatha, which he wrote to destroy the Jews who are in all the provinces of the king.* For how can I bear to see the calamity that is coming to my people? Or how can I bear to see the destruction of my kindred?" Then King Ahasuerus said to Queen Esther and to Mordecai the Jew, "Behold, I have given Esther the house of Haman, and they have hanged him on the gallows, because he intended to lay hands on the Jews.

In view of divine intervention, the king's response to Esther was steady and favorable. He gave Esther the authority to write a new decree because the previous one was sealed with the king's ring and could not be revoked. **Esther 8:8-17**,

But *you may write as you please with regard to the Jews, in the name of the king, and seal it with the king's ring, for an edict written in the name of the king and sealed with the king's ring cannot be revoked.*"

The king's scribes were summoned at that time, in the third month, which is the month of Sivan, on the twenty-third day. And *an edict was written, according to all that Mordecai commanded concerning the Jews, to the satraps and the governors and the officials of the provinces from India to Ethiopia, 127 provinces, to each province in its own script and to each people in its own language, and also to the Jews in their script and their language. And he wrote in the name of King Ahasuerus and sealed it with the king's signet ring.* Then he sent the letters by mounted couriers riding on swift horses that were used in the king's service, bred from the royal stud, saying that the king allowed the Jews who were in every city to gather and defend their lives, to destroy, to kill, and to annihilate any armed force of any people or province that might attack them, children and women included, and to plunder their goods, on one day throughout all the provinces of King Ahasuerus, on the thirteenth day of the twelfth month, which is the month of Adar. A copy of what was written was to be issued as a decree in every province, being publicly displayed to all peoples, and the Jews were to be ready on that day to take vengeance on their enemies. So the couriers, mounted on their swift horses that were used in the king's service, rode out hurriedly, urged by the king's command. And the decree was issued in Susa the citadel.

Then Mordecai went out from the presence of the king in royal robes of blue and white, with a great golden crown and a robe of fine linen and purple, and the city of Susa shouted and rejoiced. The Jews had light and gladness and joy and honor. And in every province and in every city, wherever the king's command and his edict reached, there was gladness and joy among the Jews, a feast and a holiday. And many from the peoples of the country declared themselves Jews, for fear of the Jews had fallen on them.

Attention

Attentiveness: There are three levels of attention that are needed for an intercessor to communicate with the Lord effectively. An attentive mind is usually connected to a listening and hearing ear.

Listening: It is to make a conscious effort to hear what is being said. It is the strength of divine communication and the vitality of relationship.

- Listening is an act of paying attention to somebody or something in order to hear what is being said or done.
- The act of listening is one of the qualities that an intercessor must possess in order to communicate with the Lord effectively.
- An intercessor must have a hearing ear to be able to receive from the throne of grace when presenting a matter to the Lord in the court of heaven.
- Both the intercessor and the petitioner must endeavor to pay attention to divine instructions and direction during intercessory prayer sessions.

Hearing: It is the ability to perceive sound. It is the state of catching, receiving, understanding, hearkening, getting, gathering, learning, and considering what is being said.

> **Act 12:16** But Peter continued knocking, and when they opened, they saw him and were amazed.

> **Luke 13:25** When once the master of the house has risen and shut the door, and you begin to stand outside and to knock at the door, saying, 'Lord, open to us,' then he will answer you, 'I do not know where you come from.'

> **Revelation 3:20** Behold, I stand at the door and knock. If anyone hears my voice and opens the door, I will come in to him and eat with him, and he with me.

Intercessory Communications and Conversation

- **Esther Type of Intercession:** Esther took an uncommon risk to die for her people, while she went into the realms of intercession to negotiate with the king on behalf of her people. She continued the negotiation by seeking favor, and ensuring that it was granted before she presented her case.**

- **Daniel Type of Intercessory Prayer:** When the leadership of King Nebuchadnezzar conspired against Daniel out of envy and jealousy in an attempt to dismantle his relationship with his God, Daniel prayed until Jehovah God proved himself as living and real. Daniel's prayer also disturbed the king's night sleep until the king himself could not sleep, but pleaded with the Lord to spare Daniel from being mauled by the lions. **

- **Nehemiah Type of Intercessory Prayer:** When Nehemiah heard about the broken walls of Jerusalem, he cried unto the Lord with fasting and intercessory prayer until the Lord stirred up his master the king to feel his pain and noticed his burden.**

Equipment for Intercession – Training for Knowledge and Skills
Speak to the Lord before going to war.
Ask for divine instruction and direction.
Joshua needed divine instruction to pull down the walls of Jericho.

Empowerment for Intercession – Wisdom and Application
Moses needed divine wisdom to ask the Lord for water in the wilderness

- **Intercession for Action** – Application of Rules and Regulations
- **Intercession while on the Field** – Instructions and Directions

Intercession in Action

Prayer Focus
Request for the language and dynamics of intercessory mission

Goal
Need to know how to speak the language that touches the throne of grace and mercy
Need to be able to connect with the throne of mercy for transformation of situations
Need to establish relationship for effective transmission of information
Need to maintain and sustain contact with the throne of grace and mercy
Need to utilize the dynamics of language

Prayer of Worship and Adoration
Blessed be the Lord God of heaven and earth,
The Maker and knower of all things,
You are worthy to be praised and adored.
Who is a pardoning God like you?
Who is rich in grace and mercy like you are?
Who delights not in the death of a sinner but you?
Blessings and honor belong to you.
You deserve the glory and the honor.

Prayer of Confession and Repentance
I stand on the authority of your Word in Acts 3:19 that says,
"Repent ye therefore, and be converted, that your sins may be blotted out, when the times of refreshing shall come from the presence of the Lord."
Therefore, I confess my sins of transgression and those of my family,
and ask for the power to overcome the weaknesses that have caused us to come short of the glory of Jehovah God,

So that we will no long practice nor retain iniquity in
our hearts.
O Lord, blot out or sins and enable us to experience
refreshing times in you.

Prayer of Forgiveness and Restoration

O Lord God of grace, who pardons sin and delights in mercy,
forgive our transgression and trespasses;
Let the blood of Jesus that was shed for pardon delete the
stain and stench of iniquity from our hearts;
O Lord, pardon and restore us to thy righteousness,
as your Word declares in Micah 7:18-19,
"Who is a God like unto thee, that pardoneth iniquity, and
passeth by the transgression of the remnant of his heritage? he retaineth not his anger for ever, because he
delighteth in mercy.
He will turn again, he will have compassion upon us; he will
subdue our iniquities; and thou wilt cast all their sins into the
depths of the sea."

Prayer of Petition

**O Lord, in view of your mercies and compassion,
I make petition to the throne of grace, that you
will grant me**
the language and dynamics of intercessory mission,
and teach me to communicate various requests on behalf of
the needy.
O Lord, grant me the ability to speak the language that
touches the throne of grace and mercy,
That I will be able to connect with the throne of mercy for
transformation of situations.
O Lord, enable me to establish relationship with your presence, for effective contact and transmission of information.
O Lord, grant me wisdom to maintain and sustain contact
with the throne of grace and mercy, in order to utilize the

dynamics of intercessory communications for the benefit of salvation and deliverance of humanity.
O Lord, teach me to ask and seek your will and desire, so that thy will be done on earth as it is in heaven.
O Lord, teach me to knock, so that the windows of heaven will be open unto me according to your promises.

Invocation of Blessings
O Lord God of grace and mercies,
Blessings, honor, and glory belong to you.
O Lord, consider your word in Psalm 103:2-5 that says,
"Bless the LORD, O my soul, and forget not all his benefits:
Who forgiveth all thine iniquities; who healeth all thy diseases;
Who redeemeth thy life from destruction; who crowneth thee with lovingkindness and tender mercies;
Who satisfieth thy mouth with good things; so that thy youth is renewed like the eagle's."
And let your face shine upon me.
Surround me with your divine favor and hear my cry when I call.
Intervene in all matters that I present to you,
And cover me with your feathers of protection. Amen!

Song of Motivation
Who is a Pardoning God like Thee

Great God Of Wonders! All Thy Ways
John Westley Harding
Author: Samuel Davies, 1723-1761
Musician: John Newton, 1725-1807

Scripture Nehemiah 9:17; Isaiah 55:1-9;
Daniels 9:9; Micah 7:18; Ephesians 1:7;
Psalm 77:17

1. GREAT God of wonders! all thy ways
   Display the attributes divine;
   But countless acts of pardoning grace
   Beyond thine other wonders shine:
   Who is a pardoning God like thee?
   Or who has grace so rich and free?

2. In wonder lost, with trembling joy
   We take the pardon of our God;
   Pardon for crimes of deepest dye,
   A pardon bought with Jesus's blood:
   Who is a pardoning God like thee?
   Or who has grace so rich and free?

3. Pardon-from an offended God!
   Pardon-from sin of deepest dye!
   Pardon-bestowed through Jesus's blood!
   Pardon-that brings the rebel nigh!
   Who is a pardoning God like thee?
   Or who has grace so rich and free?

4. 0 may this strange, this matchless grace,
   This God-like miracle of love,
   Fill the wide earth with grateful praise,

As now it fills the choirs above!
Who is a pardoning God like thee?
Or who has grace so rich and free?

References:

The American Heritage Dictionary of the English Language (5th ed.). (2011). Boston, MA: Houghton Mifflin Harcourt.
www.allthelyrics.com/lyrics/john_westley_harding/
www.ccg.org
www.desiringgod.org
www.meriam-webster.com/dictionary
www.nationaldayofprayer.org
www.relevantbibleteaching.com
www.thefreedictionary.com
www.thequickenedword.com

Chapter Six

Different Types of Intercessory Communications

People of every nation have a peculiar manner and approach to prayer. The nature of a people's traditional background does affect the understanding of what prayer should be and how it ought to be done. As discussed in earlier chapters of this book, prayer is communication between mankind and God, or a deity of some sort; however, the traditional background does affect a person's attitude. Therefore, the notion of different types of prayer may be susceptible to the fact that people who are used to the prophetic environment may turn to pray in a certain way. Familiarity can either motivate or discourage people from approaching intercessory prayer in a particular way.

Intercession as a Lawyer: Fundamentally, the act of intercession is like that of a lawyer or an attorney-at-law appealing cases in the court of heaven. Also, it is a system of begging for grace and mercy before the Almighty God who is also the judge of the whole universe.

If a person's belief system sees an intercessor as a beggar asking for help, then one's approach to prayer will be like that of a beggar. Similarly, if a person believes that an intercessor could play the role of an attorney-at-law to appeal cases in court on behalf of clients, then one's mode of prayer may assume the pattern of an attorney in the court of justice.

In view of this explanation, it will be relevant to discuss some of the different types of intercessory prayers that are usually practiced in different environments and are also historically biblical.

These include:

- Regular Intercession/Intercessor
- Prophetic Intercession/Intercessory Prophet
- Warfare Intercession/Intercessory Warfare
- Watchman Intercession/Intercessory Watchman

Regular Intercession/Individual Intercessor

In the realms of regular intercessory prayer, people may express a simple faith and yet obtain the desired result. The reason being that the Lord will honor his word to grant us grace and show us mercy. By virtue of his grace, the Lord may hear and listen to the cry of the innocent, and the simple-hearted persons whenever they call upon him. God is gracious and his mercies endure forever.

> **Jeremiah 33:2-3** Thus says the LORD who made the earth, the LORD who formed it to establish it—the LORD is his name: Call to me and I will answer you, and will tell you great and hidden things that you have not known.

The Burden of Intercession: Every intercessor may not be officially appointed, chosen, or ordained, yet a person may have the burden to stand in the gap for others. Sometimes, an intercessor is divinely assigned, but the Lord is keeping the person in focus until an appointed season of maturity to be presented on the stage of recognition at a certain time in a certain place. However, every intercessor must operate on legal grounds in order to gain access and pardon for the matter at stake. The fact that the Almighty God is gracious and merciful does not give an intercessor any reason to dishonor his righteousness. The Lord must be honored in all things at all times, so that the cry of a petitioner is heard, especially when an intercessor intervenes in the matter by presenting it in the appeal court of heaven.

> **James 5:16 (KJV)** Confess your faults one to another, and pray one for another, that ye may be healed. The effectual fervent prayer of a righteous man availeth much.

Human Rights Activist: In the secular world, "human rights law developed out of customs and theories that established the rights of the individuals in relation to the state. These rights were expressed in legal terms in documents such as the English Bill of Rights of 1688, the U.S. Declaration of Independence of 1776, the U.S. Bill of Rights added to the U.S. Constitution in 1789, and the French Declaration of the Rights of Man and the Citizen added to the French Constitution in 1791" (www. legal-dictionary.thefreedictionary.com).

In view of that development, there are people who operate as human rights activists. Consequently, there are attorneys who serve as human rights lawyers. The human rights activists and lawyers go to court every now and then to fight for justice on behalf of individuals and the public. Both activists and attorneys are people who formulate some form of legal grounds on which they stand to protect and defend some variation of human rights laws. They are also involved in defending some individual activities that seem contrary to their expectations and belief system.

According to the Legal-Dictionary, human rights are the "basic rights that fundamentally and inherently belong to each individual." Furthermore, it states that, "Human rights are freedoms established by custom or international agreement that impose standards of conduct on all nations. Human rights are distinct from civil liberties, which are freedoms established by the law of a particular state and applied by that state in its own jurisdiction" (www.legal-dictionary.thefreedictionary.com).

Appeal for Justice: Consequently, intercessors can be described as spiritual human rights activists who go to spiritual court on behalf of others to appeal for justice. Intercessors go to the court of heaven to appeal to God to consider a case based on the act of redemption and pardon. The purpose of the death of Jesus Christ on the cross is to buy our pardon and redeem us from the condemnation of sin.

> **John 3:17** For God did not send his Son into the world to condemn the world, but in order that the world might be saved through him. Whoever believes in him is not condemned, but whoever does not believe is condemned already, because he has not believed in the name of the only Son of God.

> **1 John 1:9** If we confess our sins, he is faithful and just to forgive us *our* sins and to cleanse us from all unrighteousness.

Application for Justice: Although the Lord is the Judge of the whole world, another part of his attributes is that he is gracious and merciful; yet the nature of his mercy cannot be taken for granted. Therefore, an intercessor must ensure that the requestor makes a conscious effort to draw nigh to God with confession of sin and repentance in order to gain the honor of divine favor. The Lord will not compromise his holiness and righteousness in the process of justice. His grace and mercy do not give us license to continue to sin or transgress his law of righteousness.

2 Chronicles 30:9 For if you return to the LORD, your brothers and your children will find compassion with their captors and return to this land. For the LORD your *God is gracious and merciful* and will not turn away his face from you, if you return to him."

Psalm 116:5 *Gracious is the LORD, and righteous; our God is merciful.*

Isaiah 30:18 Therefore *the LORD waits to be gracious to you, and therefore he exalts himself to show mercy to you.* For the LORD is a God of justice; blessed are all those who wait for him.

Joel 2:13 "Rend your hearts and not your garments." *Return to the LORD your God, for he is gracious and merciful, slow to anger,* and abounding in steadfast love; and he relents over disaster.

The Price of Intercession: At another level where innocence is betrayed, one may have to pay a price in order to access the presence of the Almighty God. The kind of price that one may be expected to pay is not the same as the price that Christ Jesus paid for the redemption of our souls. This kind of price may be related to knowledge, skillfulness, responsibility, and accountability. An attorney does not go to court to defend a case without knowledge of court proceedings and knowledge of the matter at hand. As Scripture states, "Study to shew thyself approved unto God, a workman that needeth not to be ashamed, rightly dividing the word of truth." (**2 Timothy 2:15 KJV**).

Obedience: Obedience means you agree with the word of the Lord and submit to work and walk in compliance with it with honor and respect. The act of obedience requires that one follows instruction, by observing the rules and regulations that are provided to guide and direct as required.

Disobedience: Disobedience is to insist on one's personal wants, desires, and ungodly choices that do not conform to the scriptural Word of God. A person who disregards authority and the Word of God is living in sin in defiance of truth. Although that person may still function in the office of intercession, and still see vision and prophecy, the person will not have real peace or joy in life. The person's nights will be restless as he or she will seek peace and joy in material satisfaction, instead of giving up the lifestyle of disobedience.

The price of disobedience is costly. It is a type of witchcraft as it insists on its own desires and longings. It is a spirit of covetousness that wants something that belongs to another person. The spirit of disobedience does not care about the end result of its action, so long as the person's ungodly wants and desires are selfishly satisfied.

A lady who is supposed to be an active intercessor once said that she does not care how she satisfies her needs, as long as she has prayed and seen a vision or heard a prophecy that she could have whatever she wants. In other words, she exalts human revelations and prophecies above the Word of God. This is an act of witchcraft and the sin of rebellion, which could open up illegal doors and windows for the enemy to operate in her environment. Disobedience is an act of insubordination to divine authority which grants the enemy the legal grounds to torment and harass members of one's family.

Submission: Wherever there is obedience, there is submission to authority, and compliance is easy. A submissive person is one who has surrendered his or her entire will, desires, and wishes to the Word of God. The person does not contend with the Word of God and does not exalt himself or herself above the legal authority of God.

A submissive person must be willing to yield their desires and wishes to the perfect will of God by agreeing to what Scriptures require at any time. It is an act of agreement with the word of truth in order to avoid dispute and contest over a matter by wrestling for self-will or covetous desire.

Insubordination is an act of pride and ego above the Word of God. It is the typical characteristic of Satan, the devil. It is an expression of envy and jealousy that wants to rule and ride on other people's possessions, and if possible on everyone.

Insubordination is also an act of rebellion and defiance against scriptural truth. An insubordinate person is one who refuses to obey orders or submit to authority.

A person operating in the realm of intercession must not indulge in the act of insubordination. The price of insubordination is like that of a person who indulges in the sin of witchcraft. The Word of God declares that rebellion is as the sin of witchcraft.

> **1 Samuel 15:23 (KJV)** For rebellion is as the sin of witchcraft, and stubbornness is as iniquity and idolatry. Because thou hast rejected the word of the LORD, he hath also rejected thee from being king.
>
> **Job 34:37** For he adds rebellion to his sin; he claps his hands among us and multiplies his words against God."
>
> **Jeremiah 28:16** Therefore thus says the LORD: 'Behold, I will remove you from the face of the

earth. This year you shall die, because you have
uttered rebellion against the LORD.'"

Jeremiah 29:32 Therefore thus says the LORD:
"Behold, I will punish Shemaiah of Nehelam
and his descendants. He shall not have anyone
living among this people, and he shall not see
the good that I will do to my people, declares
the LORD, for he has spoken rebellion against
the LORD."

Jeremiah 33:8 I will cleanse them from all the
guilt of their sin against me, and I will forgive
all the guilt of their sin and rebellion against me.

2 Thessalonians 2:3 Let no one deceive you in
any way. For that day will not come, unless the
rebellion comes first, and the man of lawlessness is revealed, the son of destruction,

Hebrews 3:8 *Do not harden your hearts as
in the rebellion, on the day of testing in the
wilderness.*

Humility is the quality of integrity. It is the act of being modest
and respectful. An intercession must demonstrate a high sense
of humility in the face of challenges and difficulties. An intercessor must exhibit a high quality of respect in times of trials
and temptations. Humility is the reverse side of pride.

Pride is the act of self-defense where one seeks to exalt oneself at the least opportunity to arrogate self instead of seeking
the Lord for restoration. Pride attracts shame and disgrace at a
time when one deserves honor and excellence.

An intercessor must stay away from the spirit of pride. Pride is the first characteristic of Satan the devil. Pride leads to destruction. (*See detailed discussion on pride in subsequent chapters*).

The Fear of God is to consider how God feels about a matter and the end of it thereof, instead of what you expect to gain from a situation. The fear of God keeps you from doing anything that may hurt the throne of righteousness, instead seeking your personal pride and security. It makes you aware that the end of things that is displeasing to the Spirit of Truth leads to damnation, and so you would rather please the Lord and be saved to the end.

> **Psalm 111:10** *The fear of the LORD is the beginning of wisdom*; all those who practice it have a good understanding. His praise endures forever!

> **Proverbs 1:7** *The fear of the LORD is the beginning of knowledge*; fools despise wisdom and instruction.

> **Proverbs 9:10** *The fear of the LORD is the beginning of wisdom, and the knowledge of the Holy One is insight.*

> **Exodus 18:21** Moreover, look for able men from all the people, *men who fear God, who are trustworthy and hate a bribe, and place such men over the people* as chiefs of thousands, of hundreds, of fifties, and of tens.

> **Deuteronomy 6:2** That you may fear the LORD your God, you and your son and your son's son, *by keeping all his statutes and his*

commandments, which I command you, all the days of your life, and that your days may be long.

Deuteronomy 8:6 So *you shall keep the commandments of the LORD your God by walking in his ways and by fearing him.*

Deuteronomy 10:12 "And now, Israel, *what does the LORD your God require of you, but to fear the LORD your God, to walk in all his ways, to love him, to serve the LORD your God with all your heart and with all your soul,*

2 Samuel 23:3 The God of Israel has spoken; the Rock of Israel has said to me: When one rules justly over men, ruling in the fear of God,

2 Kings 17:39 But *you shall fear the LORD your God, and he will deliver you out of the hand of all your enemies.*

Ecclesiastes 12:13 The end of the matter; all has been heard. Fear God and keep his commandments, for this is the whole duty of man.

2 Corinthians 7:1 Since we have these promises, beloved, *let us cleanse ourselves from every defilement of body and spirit, bringing holiness to completion in the fear of God.*

Ephesians 5:21 Submitting yourselves one to another in the fear of God.

Hebrews 11:7 By faith Noah, being warned by God concerning events as yet unseen, in reverent fear constructed an ark for the saving of his household. By this he condemned the world and became an heir of the righteousness that comes by faith.

Revelations 14:7 And he said with a loud voice, *"Fear God and give him glory, because the hour of his judgment has come, and worship him who made heaven and earth, the sea and the springs of water."*

Intercession in Action

Prayer Focus
Wisdom for different types of intercessory petitions

Goal
Need to understand and connect with the burden of the Lord
Need to be sensitive and attentive to intercessory burdens
Need to know how to utilize various forms of languages
needed for specific petitions
Need to learn how to appeal different type of cases in the
court of heaven
Need to be able to pay the price of intercession without mur-
muring and complaining
Need the spirit of obedience and humility to stand in the gap
for others
Need the fear of God to rule my thoughts and behavior that I
may not sin against the burden of the Lord

Prayer of Worship and Adoration
O Lord God of divine intervention,
You are the one who hears our cry and attends to our needs,
As the Word declares in **Jeremiah 33:2-3**,
"Thus says the LORD who made the earth, the LORD who
formed it to establish it—the LORD is his name: Call to me
and I will answer you, and will tell you great and hidden
things that you have not known."
Yes, Lord, you are the living One who listens to the cry of
your children.
Yes, you are the only One that hears and answers.
Great and mighty are you, O Lord most holy.

Prayer of Confession and Repentance
O Lord God most holy, we have sinned against you.
We have considered iniquity in our heart and have not obeyed
your word.

We have transgressed your commands and rebelled against the truth.
O Lord, I stand on behalf of our parents to repent from all our wickedness and rebelliousness.

Prayer of Forgiveness and Restoration:
O Lord God of grace and compassion,
You are the one that forgives and restores.
Have mercy upon us according to your word in Isaiah 1:18 that says,
"Come now, and let us reason together, saith the LORD:
though your sins be as scarlet, they shall be as white as snow;
though they be red like crimson, they shall be as wool."
O Lord, draw us into your open arms of love, and transform our souls to be like you again.

Prayer of Petition
O Lord God of mercy and compassion,
You are the living God who hears and answers our cry,
O Lord, consider your word in **Jeremiah 33:2-3,**
"Thus says the LORD who made the earth, the LORD who formed it to establish it—the LORD is his name: Call to me and I will answer you, and will tell you great and hidden things that you have not known."
Therefore, grant us the ability to understand and connect with the burden of the Lord.
Make us to be sensitive and attentive to intercessory burdens that you assign to us.
Enable us know how to utilize various forms of languages needed for specific petitions.
Teach us to learn how to appeal different types of cases in the court of heaven.
O Lord, enable us to be able to pay the price of intercession without murmuring and complaining.
Give us the spirit of obedience and humility to stand in the gap for others.

Inject us with the fear of God to rule our thoughts and
behavior, so that we may not sin against the burden
of the Lord.

Invocation of Blessings
Lord, open the windows of heaven, and pour out your bless-
ings upon us
So that you will hear us when we cry, and attend to our needs.
According to your word in **1 Thessalonians 3:11-13**,
"Now God himself and our Father, and our Lord Jesus Christ,
direct our way unto you.
And the Lord make you to increase and abound in love
one toward another, and toward all men, even as we do
toward you:
To the end he may stablish your hearts unblameable in holi-
ness before God, even our Father, at the coming of our Lord
Jesus Christ with all his saints."
Therefore, direct our ways unto yourself.
Make us to increase and abound in love toward one another.
Establish us in your hearts
That we may be unblameable in holiness before your throne.
Let your face shine upon us, and let your glory be seen
in us. Amen!

Song of Motivation:
Guide Me, O Thou Great Jehovah

The United Methodist Hymnal Number 127
Text: William Williams, 1717-1791;
trans. from the Welsh by Peter Williams and the author
Music: John Hughes, 1873-1932
Copyright status is *Public Domain*
Subject: Guidance, Supplication
Scripture: Exodus 13:21

Guide me, O Thou great *Jehovah, [*Redeemer]
Pilgrim through this barren land;
I am weak, but Thou art mighty,
Hold me with Thy pow'rful hand.
Bread of heaven, Bread of heaven,
Feed me till I want no more;
Feed me till I want no more.

Open now the crystal fountain,
Whence the healing stream doth flow;
Let the fire and cloudy pillar
Lead me all my journey through.
Strong Deliv'rer, strong Deliv'rer,
Be Thou still my Strength and Shield;
Be Thou still my Strength and Shield.

Lord, I trust Thy mighty power,
Wondrous are Thy works of old;
Thou deliver'st Thine from thralldom,
Who for naught themselves had sold:
Thou didst conquer, Thou didst conquer
Sin and Satan and the grave,
Sin and Satan and the grave.

When I tread the verge of Jordan,
Bid my anxious fears subside;
Death of death and hell's Destruction,
Land me safe on Canaan's side.
Songs of praises, songs of praises,
I will ever give to Thee;
I will ever give to Thee.

Reference:
https://library.timelesstruths.org/music/
Guide_Me_O_Thou_Great_Jehovah/

Chapter Seven

Fruit of the Spirit as Weapon

Intercessory prayer is a ministry that demands a high level of purity. Irrespective of the organizational hierarchy of the person involved, the Lord does not compromise his righteousness. Anyone entering the presence of the Lord is required to observe purity and holiness in every ramification of human existence. God is holy and expects those who lead others into his presence to observe the same.

> **Leviticus 20:26** You shall be holy to me, for I the LORD am holy and have *separated* [severed] *you from the peoples*, that you should be mine.

Weapons

A weapon is a device designed to gain advantage in a situation that is beyond one's physical ability. A weapon can also be described as ammunition for waging warfare. It is a means of defending oneself in a conflict or contest.

Military Weapons: Military weapons are dangerous and deadly. They are used to destroy an enemy and to gain advantage. Military Weapons include ammunitions. Ammunitions are some of the devices that military officers use to wage wars on battlegrounds. Such ammunitions include:

- Bullets
- Shells
- Bombs
- Missiles
- Grenades
- Ammo

Satanic/Demonic Weapons: Sexual perversion is one of the weapons that the enemy uses against the church. The enemy can use the sin of adultery and fornication to defile a minister of God and pull down his/her stronghold. Also, the enemy can use rape and incest to attack a church family or the household of a righteous person, so that his stronghold would collapse. Sexual sin can be deadly, as it brings shame and disgrace and embarrassment to a family, a community, and/or an organization.

Also, gossip, envy, strife, and anger are weapons that the enemy uses to tear down Christian communities and ministers of God. Gossip and anger are weapons of character assassination that cause an untamed tongue to disarm/defuse a righteous person and strip him of his integrity through spreading rumors.

Works of the flesh are the typical characteristics of Satan, the devil. Therefore, the enemy uses the exhibition of his character as weapons of warfare against the righteous. (See details in the subsequent chapter on *Pitfall of Intercessory Prayer*).

Prayer Weapons: There are different types of prayer as there are different types of weapons. Each type of prayer requires a particular type of weapon. All prayers are not warfare; therefore, the use of weapons is not always needed. Also, various types of warfare require different types of weapons. All weapons are not destructive. Intercessory prayer weapons are character and behavioral oriented, while weapons of spiritual warfare may be destructive as a result of violence.

Sword of the Spirit: The Word of God is the Sword of the Spirit.

- The Word of God is the major weapon that is used to wage war against the enemy.
- The Word of God is also the legal weapon with which the righteous is equipped and empowered for war.
- The Word of God is the spiritual light that guides a Christian away from borrowing from the character bank of Satan.
- The Word of God is the lamp that shines on the path of a Christian so that he/she will be able to see clearly and walk aright.
- The Word of God as a weapon enables a Christian to trample upon snakes and scorpions and is not hurt.
- The Word of God enables a Christian to walk through the valley of the shadow of death and fear no evil.

Intercessory Prayer Weapon:

In the realms of intercessory prayer, weapons are tools that give you access into the throne room of heaven to have a heart-to-heart discussion with Father God, as a child would with a father. The weapon of intercessory warfare is the fruit of the Spirit. The fruit of the Spirit is the combination of the image of Jehovah God—the Father, Son and the Holy Spirit. The fruit of the Spirit also gives us the likeness of Jesus Christ, which gives the identity of Christianity. The possession of the fruit of the Spirit is the possession of the kind of purity that consumes evil, so that darkness disappears, and the light of holiness shines to pour out mercy and grace upon the innocent sinner.

> **John 1:4-5** In him was life, and the life was the light of men. *The light shines in the darkness, and the darkness has not overcome it, and the darkness comprehended it not.*

High Priest: The fruit of the Spirit is the major weapon required to qualify a person as a high priest to enter into the throne of heaven to discuss a matter that needs the attention of God the Father for mercy and grace.

Appellant: The intercessory weapon is the fruit of the Spirit that gives an appellant the power of attorney to stand in the heavenly court of appeal to speak on behalf of others.

Presence of the Holy Spirit: One of the major purposes of the presence of the Holy Spirit in us is to enable us to live the righteous lifestyle according to the image and likeness of God our maker. The fruit of the Spirit is to instill the image of God into our character.

> **Romans 8:9** You, however, are not in the flesh but in the Spirit, if in fact the Spirit of God dwells in you. *Anyone who does not have the Spirit of Christ does not belong to him.*

> **1 Corinthians 12:13** For in one Spirit we were all baptized into one body—Jews or Greeks, slaves or free—*and all were made to drink of one Spirit.*

> **Ephesians 1:13-14** In him you also, when you heard the word of truth, the gospel of your salvation, and believed in him, *were sealed with the promised Holy Spirit,* who is the guarantee of our inheritance until we acquire possession of it, to the praise of his glory.

Fruit of the Holy Spirit

Fruitfulness is the result of growth and development. It is the sign of achievement. To be fruitful is to be productive. One of the works of the Holy Spirit is to make us fruitful as God originally created and blessed us to be fruitful.

The presence of the Holy Spirit produces the fruit of the Spirit in us. The fruit of the Spirit is the intercessory weapon needed to identify a person with Christ Jesus in the presence of the Lord and in the court of heaven.

- **Character**: The intercessory weapon is the garment of character required to enter the heavenly court of appeal.
- **Identification**: The intercessory weapon is the mark of identification that gives an intercessor the resemblance of Christ Jesus.
- **DNA**: The intercessory weapon is the fruit of the Spirit that forms the DNA of those who have been washed in the blood of Jesus Christ the Redeemer.

The fruit of the Spirit enables us to produce quality character that resists the opposing works of the flesh. It is the attribute of the Christian life. **Galatians 5:16-26** says,

> But I say, walk by the Spirit, and you will not gratify the desires of the flesh. For the desires of the flesh are against the Spirit, and the desires of the Spirit are against the flesh, for these are opposed to each other, to keep you from doing the things you want to do. But if you are led by the Spirit, you are not under the law. Now the works of the flesh are evident: sexual immorality, impurity, sensuality, idolatry, sorcery, enmity, strife, jealousy, fits of anger, rivalries, dissensions, divisions, envy, drunkenness, orgies, and things like these. I warn you, as I warned you before, that those who do such things will not inherit the kingdom of God. But the fruit of the Spirit is love, joy, peace, patience, kindness, goodness, faithfulness, gentleness,

self-control; against such things there is no law. And those who belong to Christ Jesus have crucified the flesh with its passions and desires. If we live by the Spirit, let us also keep in step with the Spirit. Let us not become conceited, provoking one another, envying one another.

The fruit of the Spirit includes:

Love/Charity/Agape:
Love is one of the greatest weapons of intercessory prayer. It is the chemistry that enables a person to share the burden on the heart of Christ Jesus. It is the chemistry that moved the Lord to die on the cross for the redemption of our souls.

God is love means love is one of the major characteristics of Jehovah God. Scripture defines love in **1 Corinthians 13:4-8** as such:

> Love is patient and kind; *love does not envy or boast;* it is not arrogant or rude. It does not insist on its own way; it is not irritable or resentful; *it does not rejoice at wrongdoing, but rejoices with the truth.* Love bears all things, believes all things, hopes all things, endures all things. Love never ends. As for prophecies, they will pass away; as for tongues, they will cease; as for knowledge, it will pass away.

Love is further described as the character of Jehovah God in **1 John 4:7-8**,

> Beloved, let us love one another, *for love is from God*, and *whoever loves has been born of God and knows God.* Anyone who does not love does not know God, *because God is love.*

Joy/Chara:

Joy is rooted in God and comes from him. Joy is deeper than happiness. Happiness is but for a moment, and fades away. Joy is like a river that flows continuously irrespective of any matter or situation that befalls a person. Trouble may come, but it does not interfere with the flow of joy that gives the assurance that the Lord is with you and will never leave nor forsake you. Joy is a constant assurance of love that flows from the heart of God and from the mountain of his holiness. Like springs of water, joy is satisfaction.

George Campbell Morgan describes joy as the "consciousness of love." According to **Psalm 144:15 (KJV)**, "Happy is that people, that is in such a case: yea, happy is that people, whose God is the LORD."

> **Nehemiah 8:10** Then he said to them, "Go your way. Eat the fat and drink sweet wine and send portions to anyone who has nothing ready, for this day is holy to our Lord. And do not be grieved, for the joy of the LORD is your strength."

> **Hebrews 12:2** Looking to Jesus, the founder and perfecter of our faith, who for the joy that was set before him endured the cross, despising the shame, and is seated at the right hand of the throne of God.

Peace/ Shalom:

Peace is the rest of mind and heart that makes one trust in the Lord without any kind of fear.

- Peace means freedom from war, from disturbance, anxiety, violence, or hostility.
- It is law and order.

- Peace is described as calmness, stillness, quietness, silence, tranquility, harmony, and serenity, agreement, amity, reconciliation,

Scripture describes Christ Jesus as the Prince of Peace.

> **Isaiah 9:6** For to us a child is born, to us a son is given; and the government shall be upon his shoulder, and *his name shall be called* Wonderful Counselor, Mighty God, Everlasting Father, *Prince of Peace*.

> **John 14:27** Peace I leave with you, *my peace I give unto you*: not as the world giveth, give I unto you. Let not your heart be troubled, neither let it be afraid.

> **Romans 15:13** May the God of hope fill you with all joy and peace in believing, so that by the power of the Holy Spirit you may abound in hope.

> **Roman 5:1** Therefore, since we have been justified by faith, we have peace with God through our Lord Jesus Christ.

Peace Offering

Lack of peace is the punishment of a sinful life and lifestyle. When a person is at fault and does seek repentance and restitution, he or she will be convicted. If the person does not yield to the conviction on time, he or she will lose the peace of God and will suffer torment from the enemy till one becomes used to sin.

Isaiah 48:22 "There is no peace," says the LORD, "for the wicked."

Sin and offence takes away peace. When a person eventually realizes the reason why there is no peace, it is advisable to offer a peace offering unto the Lord as part of atonement. Repentance is very important in the process of atonement where the peace offering is required to remove the burden of restlessness.

> **Ezekiel 45:17** It shall be the prince's duty to furnish the burnt offerings, grain offerings, and drink offerings, at the feasts, the new moons, and the Sabbaths, all the appointed feasts of the house of Israel: he shall provide the sin offerings, grain offerings, burnt offerings, *and peace offerings, to make atonement on behalf of the house of Israel.*

> **Ezekiel 46:2** The prince shall enter by the vestibule of the gate from outside, and shall take his stand by the post of the gate. The priests shall offer his burnt offering *and his peace offerings, and he shall worship* at the threshold of the gate. Then he shall go out, but the gate shall not be shut until evening.

Patience/Forbearance/Longsuffering:

Patience is the ability to hold one's temper for a long time in the midst of a difficult situation.

- It is the ability to endure pain and suffering without complaining.
- It is the ability to be slow to anger or not to go into a rage in the midst of offence.
- It is the ability to restrain oneself from taking revenge in times of trouble.

- It is the ability to show compassion in times of trial and tribulations.
- It is the ability to wait in times of delay and denial.
- It is the ability to remain calm in times of provocation without getting annoyed or upset.

Romans 9:22-23 What if God, desiring to show his wrath and to make known his power, has endured with much patience vessels of wrath prepared for destruction, in order to make known the riches of his glory for vessels of mercy, which he has prepared beforehand for glory.

Patience is:

- Endurance
- Tolerance
- Lack of complaint
- Persistence
- Fortitude
- Serenity

Kindness/Generosity:

Kindness is the act of being considerate and caring for others. It is the unique nature of God that led him to send his only begotten Son to ransom us after the fall of mankind in the Garden of Eden. It is out of the kindness of his heart that he restored fellowship to mankind even after he had been driven out of His presence.

> **Titus 3:4-7** But when the goodness and loving kindness of God our Savior appeared, *he saved us,* not because of works done by us in righteousness, but *according to his own mercy, by the washing of regeneration and renewal of the Holy Spirit,* whom he poured out on us richly

through Jesus Christ our Savior, *so that being justified by his grace we might become heirs according to the hope of eternal life.*

Romans 2:4 Or do you presume on the riches of his kindness and forbearance and patience, not knowing that *God's kindness is meant to lead you to repentance?*

Romans 11:22 Note then the kindness and the severity of God: severity [brutality/cruelty] toward those who have fallen, but God's kindness to you, provided you continue in his kindness. Otherwise you too will be cut off.

The words synonymous with kindness include:

- Compassion
- Sympathy
- Kindheartedness
- Benevolence
- Thoughtfulness
- Humanity
- Consideration
- Helpfulness

Goodness:
Goodness is motivated by the seed of righteousness. It is the demonstration of integrity that springs out of honesty and decency. Goodness is a virtue that springs out of the desire to extend kindness from a compassionate heart. It is a product of the presence of the Holy Spirit in a person's life

James 1:17 Every *good gift and every perfect gift is from above*, coming down from the Father of lights with whom there is no variation or shadow due to change.

Matthew 5:16 In the same way, let your light shine before others, *so that they may see your good works and give glory to your Father* who is in heaven.

Faithfulness:
Faithfulness is a firm belief in biblical doctrine.

- It is an unwavering belief in God
- It is a consistent trustworthiness and loyalty to a promise, duty to a person or organization.
- It is to have a sense of responsibility.
- It is an act of being devoted, committed, and dedicated with genuineness of heart
- It is to be accountable.

Faithfulness means to be:

- Authentic
- Real
- Accurate
- Truthful

Gentleness/Meekness/Modesty:
Gentleness is to have a mild and kind nature or mannerism. It is an act of being moderate in order not to hurt anybody in any kind of situation. It is to have a gracious and honorable mannerism.

Gentleness is also the ability to take an action that could cause agitation and lead to violence.
Gentleness can be described as:

- Mildness

- Placidness
- Humbleness
- Tenderness
- Mellowness
- Peacefulness
- Quietness
- Softness

Self-Control/Temperance:
Self-control is the ability to tame oneself in order to control one's own actions. It is the ability to restrain oneself from indulging in unnecessary desire and lustfulness.

- Discipline
- Willpower
- Restraint
- Strength of mind
- Strength of will

Galatians 5:16-26,

> But I say, walk by the Spirit, and you will not gratify the desires of the flesh. For the desires of the flesh are against the Spirit, and the desires of the Spirit are against the flesh, for these are opposed to each other, to keep you from doing the things you want to do. But if you are led by the Spirit, you are not under the law. Now the works of the flesh are evident: sexual immorality, impurity, sensuality, idolatry, sorcery, enmity, strife, jealousy, fits of anger, rivalries, dissensions, divisions, envy, drunkenness, orgies, and things like these. I warn you, as I warned you before, that those who do such things will not inherit the kingdom of God. But the fruit of the Spirit is love, joy, peace, patience, kindness,

goodness, faithfulness, gentleness, self-control; against such things there is no law. And those who belong to Christ Jesus have crucified the flesh with its passions and desires. If we live by the Spirit, let us also keep in step with the Spirit. Let us not become conceited, provoking one another, envying one another.

Weapon of Change:
The weapon of intercessory prayer is an instrument of change. It is an instrument that is used to reverse unpleasant situations from bad to good. It is an instrument that is used in devising solutions to all matters related to humanity.

Intercessory prayer weapon is a device to effect changes in the realm of the spirit to affect the natural. It is a key that opens impossible doors to grant uncommon access and favor to the needy. It is a weapon of uncommon favor that makes all things possible before the mercy throne through pleading the blood of our Lord and Savior Jesus Christ.

The possibilities of the weapons of intercession include the following:

- It is a device for reversing evil to goodness.
- It is a device for reversing the dying into living.
- It is a device for reversing lack into abundance.
- It is a device for reversing poverty into prosperity.
- It is a device for reversing ailment into healthiness.
- It is a device for reversing failure into success.
- It is a device for reversing joblessness into employment.
- It is a device for reversing rejection into acceptance.
- It is a device for reversing hatred into love.
- It is a device for reversing enmity into friendliness.
- It is a device for reversing a state of depression into victorious living.

Malachi 2:6 True instruction was in his mouth, and no wrong was found on his lips. He walked with me in peace and uprightness, and he turned many from iniquity.

The Realms of Weapons

- Knowledge is a weapon.
- Wisdom is a weapon.
- The Word is a weapon.

Intercession in Action

Prayer Focus
Need the Fruit of the Spirit to Wage Warfare

Goal
Need the effectiveness of the fruit of the Spirit for intercessory warfare
Need to know how to utilize the fruit of the Spirit in intercessory warfare
Need the fruit of the Spirit to stand against the enemy
Need the fruit of the Spirit to distinguish myself from evil
Need the fruit of the Spirit as weapons against ungodliness
Need the fruit of the Spirit to subdue the enemy of righteousness

Prayer of Worship and Adoration
Our Father in Heaven,
You are the King of kings and Lord of all;
Great and mighty are you over all the earth;
You deserve the glory and honor;
All praise and adoration belong to you;

Prayer of Confession and Repentance
O Lord, your Word declares in **James 4:8-10 (KJV),**
"Draw nigh to God, and he will draw nigh to you. Cleanse your hands, ye sinners; and purify your hearts, ye double minded.
Be afflicted, and mourn, and weep: let your laughter be turned to mourning, and your joy to heaviness.
Humble yourselves in the sight of the Lord, and he shall lift you up."
Therefore, we humble ourselves before the Lord,
To confess our sins of transgression and trespasses;
For we have disobeyed your word and despised your ordinances.

O Lord, we repent from our indulgences in the works of
the flesh,
That we will no longer consider iniquities in our hearts.

Prayer of Forgiveness and Restoration
O Lord, we plead forgiveness,
according to your word in **Ephesians 1:7 (KJV)** that says,
"In whom we have redemption through his blood, the forgive-
ness of sins, according to the riches of his grace."
Therefore, forgive us of all our transgressions and trespasses.
Draw us back to yourself, and restore your image and like-
ness into our body, soul, and spirit.

Prayer of Petition
O Lord, have mercy upon us and impart your character and
purpose in our very beings,
To maintain and sustain the fruit of the Holy Spirit in our
entire lives.
As we petition your throne for the fruit of the Holy Spirit to
stand against the wiles of the enemy,
O Lord, grant us effectiveness of the fruit of the Spirit for
intercessory warfare;
Teach us to know how to utilize the fruit of the Spirit in intercessory warfare;
O Lord, we need the fruit of the Spirit to distinguish ourselves from the works of the flesh.
We need the fruit of the Spirit as weapons against
ungodliness.
We need the fruit of the Spirit to subdue the enemy of
righteousness.
O Lord, revive your image in our lives, that your light may
shine in us,
So that we can subdue the powers of darkness at the mention
of the name of Jesus Christ our Lord and Redeemer.

Invocation of Blessings

137

O Lord our Father, we declare your word according to
Philippians 4:7 (KJV),
"And the peace of God, which passeth all understanding, shall keep your hearts and minds through Christ Jesus."
O Lord, hear our cry and open the floodgates of heaven and release favor unto us.
Intervene in all matters that concern us.
O Lord, let our petitions not be in vain.
I declare the blessing upon our lives according to
Deuteronomy 28:9 (KJV),
"The LORD shall command the blessing upon thee [us] in thy [our] storehouses, and in all that thou [we] settest thine [our] hand unto; and he shall bless thee [us] in the land which the LORD thy [our] God giveth thee [us].

Song of Motivation:
There Shall Be Showers Of Blessing

There Shall Be Showers Of Blessing
Words: Daniel W. Whittle, 1883; first appeared in Gospel Hymns No. 4.
Music: James McGranahan, 1883
Subject: Faith, Supplication, Encouragement, Prayer
Scripture: Ezekiel 34:26; Psalm 115:12; Genesis 32:26

1. There shall be showers of blessing:
   This is the promise of love;
   There shall be seasons refreshing,
   Sent from the Savior above.

   Refrain
   Showers of blessing,
   Showers of blessing we need:
   Mercy drops round us are falling,
   But for the showers we plead.

4. There shall be showers of blessing,
   Precious reviving again;
   Over the hills and the valleys,
   Sound of abundance of rain.

5. There shall be showers of blessing;
   Send them upon us, O Lord;
   Grant to us now a refreshing,
   Come, and now honor Thy Word.

6. There shall be showers of blessing:
   Oh, that today they might fall,
   Now as to God we're confessing,
   Now as on Jesus we call!

7. There shall be showers of blessing,
   If we but trust and obey;
   There shall be seasons refreshing,
   If we let God have His way.

Reference:
www.cyberhymnal.org/htm/t/h/thershow.htm
https://library.timelesstruths.org/music/
There_Shall_Be_Showers_of_Blessing/

Chapter Eight

Pitfalls of Intercession

aving discussed various forms of intercessory warfare in the previous chapters, it is pertinent to also consider
the importance of preserving the environment in which it
is practiced. In view of that, this chapter examines the pitfalls
that an intercessor must avoid in order to enjoy the presence
of the Lord, and also achieve the purpose of spending time to
stand in the gap.

What Is a Pitfall?

A pitfall is the snare that interferes and causes disaster in
a manner that frustrates, as in **Job 18:9 (KJV)**: "A trap seizes
him by the heel; a snare lays hold of him." Other terms for pitfall include: Drawback, consequence, hazard, and difficulty.
Pitfalls in intercessory prayer can be described as such:

* A hidden agenda, snag or a trap that creates a stumbling
  block in the realms of intercessory prayer.

Proverbs 18:7 (KJV) A fool's mouth is his ruin, and his lips
are a snare to his soul.

- It is an unsuspected source of information that may trigger confusion, hurt, disappointment, and rejection in the environment of intercessory prayer.

Proverbs 20:25 It is a snare to say rashly, "It is holy," and to reflect only after making vows.

Proverbs 21:6 The getting of treasures by a lying tongue is a fleeting vapor and a snare of death.

Proverbs 22:25 Lest you learn his ways and entangle yourself in a snare.

- It is a dangerous utterance that is not easily recognized in the environment of intercessory prayer, yet it is dangerous and perilous.

Lamentations 3:46-48 All our enemies open their mouths against us; panic and pitfall have come upon us, devastation and destruction; my eyes flow with rivers of tears because of the destruction of the daughter of my people.

Proverbs 29:25 The fear of man lays a snare, but whoever trusts in the LORD is safe.

Ecclesiastes 9:12 For man does not know his time. Like fish that are taken in an evil net, and like birds that are caught in a snare, so the children of man are snared at an evil time, when it suddenly falls upon them.

- It is to ensnare or lure an intercessor in a bad situation so that he or she will not be able to pray, or seek the Lord on behalf of others.

Job 34:30 that a godless man should not reign, that he should not ensnare the people.

Psalm 35:8 Let destruction come upon him when he does not know it! And let the net that he hid ensnare him; let him fall into it—to his destruction!

Psalm 119:61 Though the cords of the wicked ensnare me, I do not forget your law.

Proverbs 5:22 The iniquities of the wicked ensnare him, and he is held fast in the cords of his sin.

Hosea 5:1 Hear this, O priests! Pay attention, O house of Israel! Give ear, O house of the king! For the judgment is for you; for you have been a snare at Mizpah and a net spread upon Tabor.

Hosea 9:8 The prophet is the watchman of Ephraim with my God; yet a fowler's snare is on all his ways, and hatred in the house of his God.

- In summary, intercessory pitfall is the trap that the enemy sets up to disrupt the environment where purity of heart and behavior is needed to stand in the court of heaven to appeal a case before the Judge of Righteousness.

Amos 3:5 Does a bird fall in a snare on the earth, when there is no trap for it? Does a snare spring up from the ground, when it has taken nothing?

Romans 11:9 And David says, "Let their table become a snare and a trap, a stumbling block and a retribution for them;

1 Timothy 3:7 Moreover, he must be well thought of by outsiders, so that he may not fall into disgrace, into a snare of the devil.

1 Timothy 6:9 But those who desire to be rich fall into temptation, into a snare, into many senseless and harmful desires that plunge people into ruin and destruction.

2 Timothy 2:26 and they may come to their senses and escape from the snare of the devil, after being captured by him to do his will.

The Maintenance Culture: Maintenance culture is an important factor in spiritual relationship. Relationship with the Lord may be easy but not quite easy to maintain to the very end. Many people who started the destiny-oriented race, are still left behind as they struggle to lace their shoes in the middle of the race, while some are gasping for breath and seeking water to drink. Ignorance forbade them when they were supposed to have tied up their bottles to the waist as preparation for the race. Some dropped off and some died because they were either not fit or did not gain enough education and knowledge before embarking on their journey, as they assumed that everything would be supernaturally provided.

The Parable of the Ten Virgins enlightens on the importance of knowledge against ignorance.

Matthew 25:1-12,

> "Then the kingdom of heaven will be like ten virgins who took their lamps and went to meet the bridegroom. Five of them were foolish, and five were wise. For *when the foolish took their lamps, they took no oil with them*, but *the wise took flasks of oil with their lamps*. As the bridegroom was delayed, they all became drowsy and slept. But at midnight there was a cry, 'Here is the bridegroom! Come out to meet him.' Then all those virgins rose and trimmed their lamps. And the foolish said to the wise, *'Give us some of your oil, for our lamps are going out.'* But the wise answered, saying, *'Since there will not be enough for us and for you, go rather to the dealers and buy for yourselves.'* And *while they were going to buy, the bridegroom came, and those who were ready went in with him to the marriage feast, and the door was shut.* Afterward the other virgins came also, saying, 'Lord, lord, open to us.' But he answered, 'Truly, I say to you, I do not know you.'

Lack of Knowledge Is Disastrous: Lack of knowledge and education can cause serious disaster in the realms of the spirit and the natural. A disaster in the realms of the spirit can trouble one's physical environment unless there is a quick intervention. Spiritual accidents happen because people do not know the impact of their behavior in the kingdom of darkness and their personal environment.

Many people are using their spiritual weapons to fight illegal battles and cause unnecessary injuries in Christian communities. The Lord empowered us with various forms of gifts and abilities to help one another as in the case of United

Nations Peace Mission. Unfortunately, lack of knowledge and education is causing more disaster than initiating peace in the Christian environment.

> **Deuteronomy 7:16** And you shall consume all the peoples that the LORD your God will give over to you. Your eye shall not pity them, neither shall you serve their gods, for that would be a snare to you.

> **Joshua 23:13** Know for certain that the LORD your God will no longer drive out these nations before you, but they shall be a snare and a trap for you, a whip on your sides and thorns in your eyes, until you perish from off this good ground that the LORD your God has given you.

Revelation for Redemption: Our weapons are not meant to destroy the brethren in the sheepfold, but to fight against the enemy. The revelations we receive are not meant to scatter the sheepfold, or to push people into perdition. It is meant for support and encouragement. The purpose of revelation is to provide redemption for our souls. Therefore, the power of revelation must not be used to destroy the Christian body or individuals whom the revelation concerns, but be used for rescuing the perishing, healing and delivering of souls wherever man is found.

Matthew 25:13-22,

> Watch therefore, for you know neither the day nor the hour. "For it will be like a man going on a journey, who called his servants and entrusted to them his property. *To one he gave five talents, to another two, to another one, to each according to his ability.* Then he went away. He

who had received the five talents went at once and traded with them, and he made five talents more. So also he who had the two talents made two talents more. But he who had received the one talent went and dug in the ground and hid his master's money. Now after a long time the master of those servants came and settled accounts with them. And he who had received the five talents came forward, bringing five talents more, saying, 'Master, you delivered to me five talents; here I have made five talents more.' His master said to him, 'Well done, good and faithful servant. You have been faithful over a little; I will set you over much. Enter into the joy of your master.' And he also who had the two talents came forward, saying, 'Master, you delivered to me two talents; here I have made two talents more.'

Knowledge: Lack of knowledge means one has no information. Hence, one is not familiar or aware of a particular thing. Lack of knowledge is also absence of experience, whereby one has no skill in a particular area of function or performance. The absence of knowledge is also considered ignorance. Ignorance is an appropriate word that describes a situation where a person is inexperienced and unfamiliar with a situation or an environment. Lack of knowledge is not the same as lack of education.

Matthew 25:23-30,

His master said to him, 'Well done, good and faithful servant. You have been faithful over a little; I will set you over much. Enter into the joy of your master.' He also who had received the one talent came forward, saying, 'Master, I knew you to be a hard man, reaping where you did not sow, and gathering where you scattered no seed, so I was afraid, and I went and hid your talent in the ground. Here you have what is yours.' But his master answered him, 'You wicked and slothful servant! You knew that I reap where I have not sown and gather where I scattered no seed? Then you ought to have invested my money with the bankers, and at my coming I should have received what was my own with interest. So take the talent from him and give it to him who has the ten talents. For to everyone who has will more be given, and he will have an abundance. But from the one who has not, even what he has will be taken away. And cast the worthless servant into the outer darkness. In that place there will be weeping and gnashing of teeth.' **Education**: Education is related to schooling. It is an academic learning where an instruction is given and attained for knowledge in order to establish a culture of science and art in various facets of life's endeavors.

According to the Web Dictionary,

- **Education** can be described as "the imparting and acquiring of knowledge through teaching and learning, especially at a school of similar institution."
- **Knowledge** is the ability gained through education.
- **Instruction** is the training and instruction given in a particular subject, e.g. in health matters.
- **Learning Experience** is information gathered through the experience of learning—"an informative experience."
- **Study of Teaching** is "the study of the theories and practices of teaching" in order to obtain a degree in education.

- **System for Educating People** is "the system of educating in a community of society" in order to provide "jobs in education."

Your weapons are not meant to destroy the brethren, but to fight against the enemy. The revelations you receive are not meant to scatter the sheepfold, or to push people into perdition. It is meant for support and encouragement.

Matthew 25:31-46

When the Son of Man comes in his glory, and all the angels with him, then he will sit on his glorious throne. Before him will be gathered all the nations, and he will separate people one from another as a shepherd separates the sheep from the goats. And he will place the sheep on his right, but the goats on the left. Then the King will say to those on his right, "Come, you who are blessed by my Father, inherit the kingdom prepared for you from the foundation of the world. For I was hungry and you gave me food, I was thirsty and you gave me drink, I was a stranger and you welcomed me, I was naked and you clothed me, I was sick and you visited me, I was in prison and you came to me." Then the righteous will answer him, saying, "Lord, when did we see you hungry and feed you, or thirsty and give you drink? And *when did we see you a stranger and welcome you, or naked and clothe you?* And when did we see you sick or in prison and visit you?" And the King will answer them, *"Truly, I say to you, as you did it to one of the least of these my brothers, you did it to me."* Then he will say to those on his left, *"Depart from me, you cursed, into the eternal fire prepared for the devil and his angels.* For I was hungry and you gave me no food, I was thirsty and you gave me no drink, I was a stranger and you did not welcome me, naked and you did not clothe me, sick and in prison and you did not visit me." Then they also will answer, saying, "Lord, when did we see you hungry or thirsty or a stranger or naked or sick or in prison, and did not minister to you?" Then he will answer them, saying, "Truly, I say to you, as you did not do it to one of the least of these, you did not do it to me." And these will go away into eternal punishment, but the righteous into eternal life.

Deadly Sins

Deadly sins are referred to as works of the flesh or soulish characteristics. Sin in itself is an act of evil. For sin to be referred to as deadly means it is extremely fatal and dangerous. It is a type of evil that results in the end with unbearable punishment.

Works of the Flesh: Works of the flesh represent the characteristics of Satan the Father of Lies, whose final habitation is in the lake of fire (commonly known as hellfire). Some works of the flesh are in groups and interwoven. The classification of some characteristics is such that a person who practices one character is likely to possess the other.

For instance, a person who indulges in gossip will likely be a liar as well as envious. A person who expresses envy is likely to be jealous. That person would likely possess an element of strife, and keeps malice.

Scripture also tells about certain sins that the Lord hates. Both deadly sins and the ones that the Lord hates are elements of evil that interfere with intercessory prayer. This chapter will discuss how these sins affect the environment of prayer and the lives of those involved.

Six/Seven Things that the Lord Hates:

1. Haughty eyes
2. A lying tongue
3. Hands that shed innocent blood
4. A heart that devises wicked plans
5. Feet that make haste to run to evil
6. A false witness who breathes out lies
7. One who sows discord among brothers

Proverbs 6:16-19

> *There are six things that the LORD hates, seven that are*
> *an abomination to him:*
> *haughty eyes, a lying tongue,*
> *and hands that shed innocent blood,*
> *a heart that devises wicked plans,*
> *feet that make haste to run to evil,*
> *a false witness who breathes out lies,*
> *and one who sows discord among brothers.*

What are the seven deadly sins?

Whatever the Lord hates could be considered a deadly sin.

Galatians 5:16-26,

> But I say, walk by the Spirit, and you will not
> gratify the desires of the flesh. For the desires of
> the flesh are against the Spirit, and the desires
> of the Spirit are against the flesh, for these are
> opposed to each other, to keep you from doing

the things you want to do. But if you are led by the Spirit, you are not under the law. Now the works of the flesh are evident: *sexual immorality, impurity, sensuality, idolatry, sorcery, enmity, strife, jealousy, fits of anger, rivalries, dissensions, divisions, envy, drunkenness, orgies, and things like these.* I warn you, as I warned you before, that those who do such things will not inherit the kingdom of God. But the fruit of the Spirit is love, joy, peace, patience, kindness, goodness, faithfulness, gentleness, self-control; against such things there is no law. And those who belong to Christ Jesus have crucified the flesh with its passions and desires.

If we live by the Spirit, let us also keep in step with the Spirit. Let us not become conceited, provoking one another, envying one another.

- **Gossip:**

Gossip is a terrible weapon of destruction. It is to talk about everything you receive in prayer with people. It is the practice of using your gift to cast down other people, and to relegate them to nothing, because the Lord showed you their challenges or weaknesses.

The tongue of the serpent: the tongue of the serpent is like that of scissors. It cuts down and publishes false news. It turns good into evil and turns evil into destruction.

Indulgence: Gossip is the act of saying negative things or to deliberately misrepresent information about someone. The gossiper is aware that whatever is being said ought to be kept secret, otherwise the personality involved will not be happy and information may create a displeasing atmosphere, some form of tension, a cold war, or retaliatory mission as a result of hurt.

Gossip is considered unconfirmed rumors, whispers, canards, tidbits, empty talk, etc.

According to the Hebrew Old Testament translation, gossip is the act of revealing secrets. The gossiper is "one who reveals secrets, one who goes about as a talebearer or scandal-monger." It also describes a person who engages in gossip as one "who has privileged information about people and proceeds to reveal that information to those who have no business knowing it" (www.got question.org).

Elements of Gossip

There are various types of conversation that may be classified as gossip and also mistaken for gossip. In every situation of gossip there are certain elements to be considered before the conversation could be classified as gossip.

Elements of gossip include most or some of the following:

- **Derogatory Remark**: A written or spoken utterance that is made to disparage or belittle a person whose integrity is supposed to be positively complimented. It is to express a deprecating or critical opinion about someone. A derogatory remark is offensive and insulting and could cause demotion or rejection even where a person deserves honor.
  Caution: Intercessors must be careful not to inject derogatory remarks into the language of spiritual communication. The language of intercessory prayer must be pure as the presence of the Lord is Holy.
- **Negative Comment**: A negative comment is an expression of opposition that is consciously or unconsciously

meant to disapprove of someone. A negative statement can be depressive, harmful, damaging, and destructive. It could lead to a state of denial or refusal so that a person may not be able to be progressive or prosper in life. **Caution**: Intercessors must not take prayer points or revelation received personally. They must ask the Lord questions to understand the meaning of a revelation that may appear negative. They must not share such revelation or prayer points with individuals or people who were not part of the team.

- **Deliberate Slander**: Slander is a defamatory statement that is an expression of character assassination. It is a deliberate attempt to insult and defame a person, so that the one will suffer rejection where honor and elevation is apparent. Slander is a false statement. It is malicious and has the tendency of damaging a person's reputation.

Psalm 50:20 You sit and speak against your brother; you slander your own mother's son.

Proverbs 10:18 The one who conceals hatred has lying lips, and whoever utters slander is a fool.

Proverbs 30:10 *Do not slander a servant to his master, lest he curse you, and you be held guilty.*

Ezekiel 22:9 There are men in you who slander to shed blood, and people in you who eat on the mountains; they commit lewdness in your midst.

Matthew 15:19 For out of the heart come evil thoughts, murder, adultery, sexual immorality, theft, false witness, slander.

Caution: Intercessors are called to pray by making appeals to the Lord to change a situation. They are not called to destroy or defame anyone but the enemy. Intercessors must avoid friendly fires, otherwise the enemy will gain entrance and the camp of the righteous will be invaded and divided.

Psalm 15:1-3 A Psalm of David.

O LORD, who shall sojourn in your tent?
Who shall dwell on your holy hill?
He who walks blamelessly and does what is right
and speaks truth in his heart;
who does not slander with his tongue
and does no evil to his neighbor,
nor takes up a reproach against his friend;

- **Premeditated Utterance:** When a person intentionally presents a false prayer request to launch a malicious attack on someone. An envious or jealous heart may deliberately launch a missile attack on an intercessory group by presenting a malicious prayer request. Such prayer points are false and baseless and waste of time and not real. The prayers are never answered and the intercessors become confused.

  Exodus 20:16 You shall not bear false witness against your neighbor.

  Caution: The intercessory group must try to investigate some of the prayer points that they receive. Spiritual and physical investigation is necessary in order to avoid spiritual attacks on the intercessors.
- **Expression of envy and jealousy**: Some prayer requests are produced out of envy and jealousy. Intercessors need the gift of discerning of spirits to deal with some

of the requests that are presented. Bear in mind that the Ten Commandments warned us:

Exodus 20:17 "You shall not covet your neighbor's house; you shall not covet your neighbor's wife, or his male servant, or his female servant, or his ox, or his donkey, or anything that is your neighbor's."

Caution: Do not go into the court room of intercession if you are not sure of the information presented to you. Endeavor to interview the applicant to clarify the intention of the request.

Gossiper: A person who indulges in gossip directly or indirectly can be described as:

- **Betrayer**: someone who goes against a promise or acts contrary to a vow by sharing secrets.
- **Tattletale**: someone who gossips carelessly without being cautious of the repercussions.
- **Tattler**: someone who gossips recklessly without thinking about the effect or end result.
- **Taleteller**: someone who spread rumors collected from gossips.
- **Sneak**: someone who goes around in a secretive way like a thief to share gossips.
- **Snitch**: someone who acts as an informer to give away information to authorities secretly (spy/snitcher/informer).
- **Backbiter**: someone who slanders by making a spiteful remark or unfavorable comments.

Different Types of Gossip

There are various types of conversation that may not necessarily be gossip if the elements of gossip could be well avoided. However, if a report about somebody's error or mistake is presented with various elements of gossip then the information could be classified as such.

- **Intercessory Discussion**: A group of intercessors are sometimes supposed to carefully examine certain prayer requests that are submitted to them.

  - This is to ensure that a subject of gossip is not included.
  - The purpose of the discussion is to ensure that all the team members understand the necessary details required to make petition before the Lord.

- **Betrayer of Trust**: Unfortunately, some people involved in intercessory prayer are flippant and betrayers who do not know how to keep information relayed to them for prayer. Once they hear or see something, they cannot stay still until they have shared the information with someone. As a result of such leaking mouth or loose lips, they share people's business with others without permission. It does not matter whether the information is good or bad. Any subject discussed on a prayer table must be kept with respect. The prayer request or petition must be sealed in the bottle of tears and placed in the heart of intercession and in the mercy throne room. Otherwise, the enemy may gain access to the information, steal it, and use it to whip the petitioner.

Proverbs 21:23 Whoever keeps his mouth and his tongue keeps himself out of trouble.

Discussion of a prayer topic or request cannot be classified as gossip if the intercessors avoid the use of the elements
of gossip—negative comments and derogatory reports—and
avoid rumor mongering or sharing the matter with other people
as indicated earlier in this chapter.

Also, intercessors must endeavor to keep intercessory discussions out of the ears of the public, especially where individuals are concerned. Some people are sensitive and are easily
offended irrespective of the type of information. Whether the
details are good or bad, they easily feel rejected and dishon-
ored if anything concerning them is known or discussed by a
third party. The fact that information presented for intercession
became a public matter makes it gossip.

> **Proverbs 20:19** Whoever goes about slandering
> reveals secrets; therefore *do not associate with*
> *a simple babbler.*

Therefore, intercessors must not share revelation received
from an individual applicant or requestor with anyone outside the team. To discuss such a personal request without permission would be considered gossip. Prayer requests should
not be gossip material and intercessors must not indulge in
tale-bearing.

Proverbs 18:7-9

> *A fool's mouth is his ruin,*
> *and his lips are a snare to his soul.*
> The words of a whisperer are like delicious morsels;
> they go down into the inner parts of the body.
> *Whoever is slack in his work is a brother to him who*
> *destroys.*

Leadership Discussion: At every level of leadership organization, there are various types of discussion that may sound

positive and negative. Leadership is predominantly about human management. Wherever humans are supervised, there is a tendency for some to misbehave and others to do well. No matter the situation, whatever is done, right or wrong, will be analyzed and criticized. Both the individual workers and the products will be examined and reported for accomplishment and achievements in order to forge ahead. Consequently, the process of discussion may attract good and/or bad reports.

Even if there is a tendency to degrade or fail someone for their inabilities or weaknesses, a positive language could be used to encourage, in order to avoid depressive results. Sharing negative results or comments about someone may be considered gossip, if some elements of gossip are spotted.

1Timothy 5:9-15,

> Let a widow be enrolled if she is not less than sixty years of age, having been the wife of one husband, and having a reputation for good works: if she has brought up children, *has shown hospitality, has washed the feet of the saints, has cared for the afflicted, and has devoted herself to every good work.* But refuse to enroll younger widows, for when their passions draw them away from Christ, they desire to marry and so *incur condemnation* for having abandoned their former faith. Besides that, *they learn to be idlers*, going about from house to house, and not only idlers, but also *gossips and busybodies, saying what they should not.* So I would have younger widows marry, bear children, manage their households, and *give the adversary no occasion for slander. For some have already strayed after Satan.*

Church Gossip: Many people have run away from certain church gatherings because of talebearers. Many are constantly on the go, moving from one church to the other, seeking a refuge from the talebearers who know everything about everyone are ready to broadcast the unhealthy news report to whoever has itching ears.

Sometimes, certain prayer warriors and supposed intercessors are witches and agents from the kingdom of darkness. Some of them may show awkward zealousness as they put the intercessors on the edge as though we need to perform certain rituals to attract the presence of the Lord in certain matters.

Church gossipers are often not interested in seeking the will of the Lord concerning a matter or a request. They are also not interested in prayer for the salvation of souls. They would want to drain you out of prayer with unnecessary rituals, and methods so that you are easily exhausted without result.

Proverbs 11:12-14,

> Whoever belittles his neighbor lacks sense,
> but a man of understanding remains silent.
> *Whoever goes about slandering reveals secrets,*
> *but he who is trustworthy in spirit keeps a thing covered.*
> Where there is no guidance, a people falls,
> but in an abundance of counselors there is safety.

Departmental Discussion: Most church organizations and ministries are departmentalized to enable easy performances according to needs and individual abilities. Sometimes, instead of doing the work that brought them together, people have opened the doors of their hearts to gossip. The information and the activities they work with have been turned into weapons of gossip. This kind of tale bearing has interfered with many good works as people were discouraged to hear certain conversation or see how activities are performed.

Scripture describes the people who indulge in the act of gossip as such: **Romans 1:29-32**,

> They were filled with all manner of unrighteous-
> ness, evil, covetousness, malice. They are full of
> envy, murder, strife, deceit, maliciousness. They
> are gossips, slanderers, haters of God, insolent,
> haughty, boastful, inventors of evil, disobedient
> to parents, foolish, faithless, heartless, ruthless.
> Though they know God's righteous decree that
> those who practice such things deserve to die,
> they not only do them but give approval to those
> who practice them.

Caution: Gossip is a weapon that the enemy uses to tear down church organizations and relationships. Disobedience is one of the major sins that creates a loophole or an open door for the enemy to gain entrance into a Christian community or environment.

- Disobedience is the spirit that conquered mankind in the Garden of Eden.
- Disobedience is the root cause of separation between mankind and the Lord.
- Disobedience is the blockage in spiritual communication with the Lord.
- Disobedience caused mankind to lose the original blessing of fruitfulness and multiplication.
- Disobedience opens the door for the enemy to enter a camp with false rumors that lead to gossip.
- Disobedience gives room to suspicion that creates insecurity and lack of trust.

When you walk with the Lord and obey his Word, gossip will not have a place in your life and environment. Whenever you transgress the Word of God, the enemy will enter your environment and make a mess of your personality. Obedience is better than sacrifice. No prophetic utterance or offering can cure the sin of disobedience until you return to the Lord with purity of heart and obedience. **1 Samuel 15:22-23 (KJV),**

And Samuel said, Hath the LORD *as great* delight in burnt offerings and sacrifices, as in obeying the voice of the LORD? *Behold, to obey is better than sacrifice, and to hearken than the fat of rams. For rebellion is as the sin of witchcraft, and stubbornness is as iniquity and idolatry.* Because thou hast rejected the word of the LORD, he hath also rejected thee from being king.

Lure for Gossip

There are certain things that stir up gossip in an environment. Gossip is usually caused by an act of immorality and ungodly behavior.

Anytime two persons of the opposite sex start to relate as though they are married when they are actually not, without properly establishing their relationship as required by customs and traditions, gossip will be stirred up. The initial gossip would usually focus on curiosity. People want to know if the relationship is based on legal grounds. As soon as it is detected there is some form of illegality about the relationship, the gossip will open up a rumor like a wild bush fire. All kinds of matters will arise, as people will become to use the affairs to sell and complement other products. Enemies will arise and hatred will develop as a result.

- **Envy/Jealousy:**
  Envy is to think that you are better than another person or other people. Envy makes you pride yourself as though you deserve the best rather than any other person. It makes you run down other people's achievement in order to obstruct or disrupt progress. It is a kind

of selfish behavior that does not appreciate other people's blessings.

What Is Envy? Envy is a feeling of resentfulness, whereby one desires to have another person's possessions, qualities or endowments. Envy makes a person discontented, so that one would be longing for other people's spouses, children, houses, or anything. An envious person will do anything to get whatever he or she wants even if it is unlawful, illegal, or ungodly.

Stanford Encyclopedia of Philosophy describes it thus: "Envy is a complex and puzzling emotion. It is, notoriously, one of the seven deadly sins. It is very commonly charged with being (either typically or universally) unreasonable, irrational, imprudent, vicious, or wrong to feel. With very few exceptions, the ample philosophical literature defending the rationality and evaluative importance of emotions explicitly excludes envy and a few other nasty emotions as irredeemable" (www.plato. stanford.edu).

Envy is also described as an emotion which "occurs when a person lacks another's superior quality, achievement, or possession and either desires it or wishes that the other lacked it" (Parrott, W.G. & Smith, R.H., 1993).

Envy is among the seven deadly sins listed in certain biblical documents. Both envy and jealousy are deadly emotional expressions that have torn relationships apart and also caused annihilation of lives. Many people are in debt and in illegal relationships because of envy—always longing to have everything that they ever set their eyes on. Yet they don't know how to manage their finances or their debt.

The Bible tells of many stories related to envy:

- Cain killed his brother Cain out of envy (Genesis 4).
- Saul attempted to kill David because of envy.
- Rachel envied Leah because of infertility, when she could not have children.

- Haman envied Mordecai's promotion.
- Joseph was sold into slavery because his brothers were envious and jealous of him.
- The Chief Priest, the Pharisees and Sadducees were envious of Jesus and his disciples because of their abilities to perform miracles with signs and wonders following.

An envious heart cannot function effectively in the place of intercession. Whenever an envious heart sees a good revelation about someone or persons, he/she will either defame the revelation to sound negatively, or claim the message for themselves, or superimpose themselves into the picture as though they made it happen. The state of envy will often contaminate the message laid on the altar of intercession.

Envy has been identified with the snake—serpentine spirit. In the Garden of Eden, the serpent was envious of the wealth that the Lord had bestowed upon mankind through Adam and Eve. The serpent deceived them as he tricked them into disobeying the Lord so that he could exchange his loss with the poverty with wealth.

Envy has also been described as "the desire for others' traits, status, abilities, or situation" (www.deadly.com).

> **1 Peter 2:1-3** So put away all malice and all deceit and hypocrisy and envy and all slander. Like newborn infants, long for the pure spiritual milk, that by it you may grow up into salvation— if indeed you have tasted that the Lord is good.

- **Jealousy:**
  Jealousy is when you feel you are the right person to be in charge and want to have control over things at all times. Jealousy makes you want to control other people's personal lives and activities. It makes you feel that

you have a better idea and ability than others. A jealous person does not allow other people to express themselves or feelings. They easily relegate other people's ability and achievement unless they are involved.

What is Jealousy? Jealousy is a spirit of competition. It expresses fear of replacement. It is anxious and suspicious. It vies of complete devotion. It is relationship prone as it cuddles with affection and is love oriented. A jealous person easily creates a sense of rivalry, enmity, contention, and challenge.

Both envy and jealousy are emotional expressions of feelings. Many people use the two words interchangeably as though they mean the same thing. According to Dr. Yochi Cohern-Charash, of Baruch College and the City University of New York, "One reason people often mistaken the two for each other is because jealousy reactions and envious reactions often look similar." Jealousy is an expression of fear of losing something, while envy is an expression of desiring to possess something (www.huffingtonpost.com).

- **Malice/cold war/withdrawal:**
  Malice is a deliberate intention to cause harm or do evil to somebody. It is a deep expression of hatred that makes a person exhibit cruelty and nastiness. A person with a malevolent heart is usually openly mischievous, as he or she may consciously demonstrate wickedness or spite without an excuse. It is either expressed in speaking, in writing, implied or inferred.

The presence of malice causes a cold war as the parties involved would usually withdraw from active relationship and communication flow.

According to the law dictionary, "Malice is the condition of the mind which shows a heart regardless of social duty and fatally bent on mischief, the existence of which is inferred from acts committed or words spoken" (Harris v. State, 8 Tex. App. 109). It is a total disregard for another person's wellbeing. (www.thelawdictionary.org)

> **Psalm 41:5** My enemies say of me in malice, "When will he die, and his name perish?"

> **Psalm 73:8** They scoff and speak with malice; loftily they threaten oppression.

> **Matthew 22:18** But Jesus, aware of their malice, said, "Why put me to the test, you hypocrites?

> **Romans 1:29** They were filled with all manner of unrighteousness, evil, covetousness, malice. They are full of envy, murder, strife, deceit, maliciousness. They are gossips,

> **1 Corinthians 5:8** Let us therefore celebrate the festival, not with the old leaven, the leaven of malice and evil, but with the unleavened bread of sincerity and truth.

> **Ephesians 4:31** Let all bitterness and wrath and anger and clamor and slander be put away from you, along with all malice.

> **Colossians 3:8** But now you must put them all away: anger, wrath, malice, slander, and obscene talk from your mouth.

> **Titus 3:3** For we ourselves were once foolish, disobedient, led astray, slaves to various passions and pleasures, passing our days in malice and envy, hated by others and hating one another.

1 Peter 2:1 So put away all malice and all deceit and hypocrisy and envy and all slander.

Malice is a premeditated evil that is deliberately carried out to effect evil. Haman is a typical character of a mischievous person who intentionally planned to annihilate the Jews in Persia. **Esther 3:1-15,**

> After these things King Ahasuerus promoted Haman the Agagite, the son of Hammedatha, and advanced him and set his throne above all the officials who were with him. And all the king's servants who were at the king's gate bowed down and paid homage to Haman, for the king had so commanded concerning him. But Mordecai did not bow down or pay homage. Then the king's servants who were at the king's gate said to Mordecai, "Why do you transgress the king's command?" And when they spoke to him day after day and he would not listen to them, they told Haman, in order to see whether Mordecai's words would stand, for he had told them that he was a Jew. And when Haman saw that Mordecai did not bow down or pay homage to him, Haman was filled with fury. But he disdained to lay hands on Mordecai alone. So, as they had made known to him the people of Mordecai, Haman sought to destroy all the Jews, the people of Mordecai, throughout the whole kingdom of Ahasuerus. In the first month, which is the month of Nisan, in the twelfth year of King Ahasuerus, they cast Pur (that is, they cast lots) before Haman day after day; and they cast it month after month till the twelfth month, which is the month of Adar. Then Haman said to King Ahasuerus, *"There is a certain people*

*scattered abroad and dispersed among the peo-
ples in all the provinces of your kingdom. Their
laws are different from those of every other
people, and they do not keep the king's laws, so
that it is not to the king's profit to tolerate them.
If it please the king, let it be decreed that they be
destroyed, and I will pay 10,000 talents of silver
into the hands of those who have charge of the
king's business, that they may put it into the
king's treasuries." So the king took his signet
ring from his hand and gave it to Haman the
Agagite, the son of Hammedatha, the enemy of
the Jews. And the king said to Haman, "The
money is given to you, the people also, to do
with them as it seems good to you."*

Then the king's scribes were summoned on the
thirteenth day of the first month, and an edict,
according to all that Haman commanded, was
written to the king's satraps and to the governors over all the provinces and to the officials
of all the peoples, to every province in its own
script and every people in its own language. It
was written in the name of King Ahasuerus and
sealed with the king's signet ring. Letters were
sent by couriers to all the king's provinces with
instruction to destroy, to kill, and to annihilate
all Jews, young and old, women and children, in
one day, the thirteenth day of the twelfth month,
which is the month of Adar, and to plunder their
goods. A copy of the document was to be issued
as a decree in every province by proclamation
to all the peoples to be ready for that day. The
couriers went out hurriedly by order of the king,
and the decree was issued in Susa the citadel.

And the king and Haman sat down to drink, but the city of Susa was thrown into confusion.

The Lord does not tolerate malice. Ezekiel pronounced the following judgment upon the nations that keep malice. **Ezekiel 25:1-17,**

> The LORD said to Moses, "Speak to the people of Israel, that they take for me a contribution. From every man whose heart moves him you shall receive the contribution for me. And this is the contribution that you shall receive from them: gold, silver, and bronze, blue and purple and scarlet yarns and fine twined linen, goats' hair, tanned rams' skins, goatskins, acacia wood, oil for the lamps, spices for the anointing oil and for the fragrant incense, onyx stones, and stones for setting, for the ephod and for the breastpiece. And let them make me a sanctuary, that I may dwell in their midst. Exactly as I show you concerning the pattern of the tabernacle, and of all its furniture, so you shall make it.

> "They shall make an ark of acacia wood. Two cubits and a half shall be its length, a cubit and a half its breadth, and a cubit and a half its height. You shall overlay it with pure gold, inside and outside shall you overlay it, and you shall make on it a molding of gold around it. You shall cast four rings of gold for it and put them on its four feet, two rings on the one side of it, and two rings on the other side of it. You shall make poles of acacia wood and overlay them with gold. And you shall put the poles into the rings on the sides of the ark to carry the ark by them. The poles shall remain in the rings of the ark;

they shall not be taken from it. And you shall put into the ark the testimony that I shall give you. You shall make a mercy seat of pure gold. Two cubits and a half shall be its length, and a cubit and a half its breadth."

- **Unforgiveness/Retaliation**:
  Retaliation is the action of harming someone because they have offended you. It is a system of paying evil with evil. It has been described as the basis for discrimination and rejection in the public sector.

A Christian who refuses to forgive is disrespecting the purpose of Christ's death on the cross of Calvary. Whenever a Christian assumes that it is impossible to forgive and let go, the enemy gains advantage and causes that person unbearable heart pain. Forgiveness brings healing and restoration, while unforgiveness causes rejection, frustration, and depression. A heart that refuses to forgive automatically seeks retaliation, as it expects evil to befall the person that has caused the pain.

> **Leviticus 19:18** You shall not take vengeance or bear a grudge against the sons of your own people, but you shall love your neighbor as yourself: I am the LORD.

> **Proverbs 20:22** Do not say, "I will repay evil"; wait for the LORD, and he will deliver you.

> **Proverbs 24:29** Do not say, "I will do to him as he has done to me; I will pay the man back for what he has done."

Retaliation is a type of revenge or retribution whereby you find it difficult to forgive when you feel offended. Other words for retaliation include: reprisal, revenge, vengeance, retribution, and punishment. **Deuteronomy 23:7-8,**

> You shall not abhor an Edomite, for he is your brother. You shall not abhor an Egyptian, because you were a sojourner in his land. Children born to them in the third generation may enter the assembly of the LORD.

Return to sender: Return to sender is a prayer of retaliation which negates the expression of love and forgiveness. Christ Jesus teaches against retaliation in **Matthew 5:38-42,**

> You have heard that it was said, "An eye for an eye and a tooth for a tooth." But I say to you, Do not resist the one who is evil. But if anyone slaps you on the right cheek, turn to him the other also. And if anyone would sue you and take your tunic, let him have your cloak as well. And if anyone forces you to go one mile, go with him two miles. Give to the one who begs from you, and do not refuse the one who would borrow from you.

When you offer the "Return to Sender" type of prayer, you are practically negating the power of God from your life. You are performing an illegal action which can cause you unbearable repercussion.

> **Romans 12:17** Repay no one evil for evil, but give thought to do what is honorable in the sight of all.

> **1 Thessalonians 5:15** See that no one repays anyone evil for evil, but always seek to do good to one another and to everyone.

How to Forgive

In order to forgive, especially when it seems impossible and you feel so much pain that sometimes causes you to cry, just look at the cross of Jesus Christ.

- See how the Lord was pierced on his side
- See how he was bruised for your sake.
- See how he shed his blood for your sake.
- Just exchange your pain with his.
- Turn over your pain to him.
- Let the shedding of his blood become meaningful to you.
- Let the blood wash away your pain and you would be healed.

1 Peter 3:9 Do not repay evil for evil or reviling for reviling, but on the contrary, bless, for to this you were called, that you may obtain a blessing.

1 Peter 4:8 Above all, keep loving one another earnestly, since love covers a multitude of sins.

Scripture also warns us to be cautious of false prophecy related to seeking vengeance against any enemy.

Jeremiah 29:7-9 But seek the welfare of the city where I have sent you into exile, and pray to the LORD on its behalf, for in its welfare you will find your welfare. For thus says the LORD of hosts, the God of Israel: Do not let your prophets and your diviners who are among you deceive you, and do not listen to the dreams that they dream, for it is a lie that they are prophesying to you in my name; I did not send them, declares the LORD.

Pretenders/Snakes in the Grass:

A pretentious person is an inventor of falsehood and sham. Such a person makes up imaginary stuff as if it is real. Someone who makes false claim to present as truth. A pretentious person is a snake in the grass.

Other words for *pretend* include: assume, cheat, impersonate, fudge, deceive, beguile, counterfeit, hypocrite, and dupe.

Scripture describes the act of pretends as such:

> **James 1:26** If anyone thinks he is religious and does not bridle his tongue but deceives his heart, this person's religion is worthless.

Isaiah 29:13-14

> And the Lord said:
> "Because this people draw near with their mouth
>   and honor me with their lips,
> while their hearts are far from me,
> and their fear of me is a commandment taught
> by men, therefore, behold, I will again
> do wonderful things with this people,
> with wonder upon wonder;
> and the wisdom of their wise men shall perish,
> and the discernment of their discerning men
> shall be hidden."

Matthew 7:21-23

Not everyone who says to me, "Lord, Lord," will enter the kingdom of heaven, but the one who does the will of my Father who is in heaven. On that day many will say to me, "Lord, Lord, did we not prophesy in your name, and cast out demons in your name, and do many mighty works in your name?" And then will I declare to them, "I never knew you; depart from me, you workers of lawlessness." Everyone then who hears these words of mine and does them will be like a wise man who built his house on the rock.

2 Corinthians 11:1-5

I wish you would bear with me in a little foolishness. Do bear with me! For I feel a divine jealousy for you, since I betrothed you to one husband, to present you as a pure virgin to Christ. But I am afraid that as the serpent deceived Eve by his cunning, your thoughts will be led astray from a sincere and pure devotion to Christ. For if someone comes and proclaims another Jesus than the one we proclaimed, or if you receive a different spirit from the one you received, or if you accept a different gospel from the one you accepted, you put up with it readily enough. Indeed, I consider that I am not in the least inferior to these super-apostles.

- **Lust/Goat**:

Lust is a strong desire or appetite for sexual affection with someone with whom one has no marital association. Lust is a spirit of greed that causes someone to go after another person's possession with no regard for the repercussion of its selfish desires. Lust is intolerant, shameless, and fearless when it longs to fulfill a desire. A lustful attitude is comparable to the behavior of a goat.

Scripture warns against the act of lust:

- It is an envious desire or longing for what belongs to another person.
- It is a covetous spirit that has no respect for the fear of God.

- It has no regard for the consequences of its action.

Exodus 20:14 You shall not commit adultery.

Exodus 20:17 You shall not covet your neighbor's house; you shall not covet your neighbor's wife, or his male servant, or his female servant, or his ox, or his donkey, or anything that is your neighbor's.

Job 31:11-12 For that would be a heinous crime; that would be an iniquity to be punished by the judges; for that would be a fire that consumes as far as Abaddon, and it would burn to the root all my increase.

Matthew 5:28 But I say to you that everyone who looks at a woman with lustful intent has already committed adultery with her in his heart.

- **Gluttony/Pig**

It is the habit of eating and drinking excessively. It is an act of greediness. Many people do not consider gluttony as sin, yet it has been described as one of the "seven deadly sins."

According to the Ethics & Religious Liberty Commission, gluttony applies to anything that is done in excess whereby one lacks the ability for self-control: "The true danger of gluttony is not that it will lead to flabby waistlines but it will lead to flabby souls. ... The habit of the body can have profound effects on the sanctification of our spirit."

A report from the commission also states that "If we are unable to control our eating habits, we are probably also unable to control other habits, such as those of the mind (lust, covetousness, anger) and unable to keep our mouths from gossip or strife" (www.erlc.com).

Also, Scripture warns against gluttony as greediness:

Proverbs 23:1-3, 6-8, 20-21

When you sit down to eat with a ruler,
observe carefully what is before you,
and put a knife to your throat
if you are given to appetite.
Do not desire his delicacies,
for they are deceptive food.
Do not eat the bread of a man who is stingy;
do not desire his delicacies,
for he is like one who is inwardly calculating.
"Eat and drink!" he says to you,
but his heart is not with you.
You will vomit up the morsels that you have eaten,
and waste your pleasant words.
Be not among drunkards
or among gluttonous eaters of meat,
for the drunkard and the glutton will come to poverty,
and slumber will clothe them with rags.

Proverbs 28:7 The one who keeps the law is a son with understanding, but a companion of gluttons shames his father.

- Christ Jesus was falsely accused of being a glutton.

Matthew 11:19 The Son of Man came eating and drinking, and they say, "Look at him! A glutton and a drunkard, a friend of tax collectors and sinners!" Yet wisdom is justified by her deeds.

• The spirit of gluttony causes laziness.

Titus 1:12 One of the Cretans, a prophet of their own, said, "Cretans are always liars, evil beasts, lazy gluttons."

• **Greed/Toad**

It is a strong desire for more of something beyond what is needed. It is deliberately wanting more than is actually needed with regards to material things. It is an intense and selfish desire for something.

Greed is the spirit of the toad and it is self-indulgence.

Ephesians 4:19 They have become callous and have given themselves up to sensuality, greedy to practice every kind of impurity.

Proverbs 30:20-23,

This is the way of an adulteress:
she eats and wipes her mouth
and says, "I have done no wrong."
Under three things the earth trembles;
under four it cannot bear up:
a slave when he becomes king,
and a fool when he is filled with food;
an unloved woman when she gets a husband,
and a maidservant when she displaces her mistress.

Love of Money: Greed can also be described as excessive love for money and material wealth.

> **Hebrews 13:5** Keep your life free from love of money, and be content with what you have, for he has said, "I will never leave you nor forsake you."

> **Proverbs 28:25** A greedy man stirs up strife, but the one who trusts in the LORD will be enriched.

> **Ecclesiastes 5:10** He who loves money will not be satisfied with money, nor he who loves wealth with his income; this also is vanity.

> **Luke 12:15** And he said to them, "Take care, and be on your guard against all covetousness, for one's life does not consist in the abundance of his possessions."

> **Matthew 6:24** No one can serve two masters, for either he will hate the one and love the other, or he will be devoted to the one and despise the other. You cannot serve God and money.

Greediness causes worldliness.

1 John 2:15-17,

> Do not love the world or the things in the world. If anyone loves the world, the love of the Father is not in him. For all that is in the world—the desires of the flesh and the desires of the eyes and pride of life—is not from the Father but is from the world.

17 And the world is passing away along with its desires, but whoever does the will of God abides forever.

Ministers and Leaders: Ministers are specifically warned to stay away from greediness, as this can affect and destroy them. **First Timothy 6:9-11,**

> But those who desire to be rich fall into temptation, into a snare, into many senseless and harmful desires that plunge people into ruin and destruction. For the love of money is a root of all kinds of evils. It is through this craving that some have wandered away from the faith and pierced themselves with many pangs. But as for you, O man of God, flee these things. Pursue righteousness, godliness, faith, love, steadfastness, gentleness.

> **Titus 1:7** For an overseer, as God's steward, must be above reproach. He must not be arrogant or quick-tempered or a drunkard or violent or greedy for gain,

Greediness is a sin that excludes one from the presence of the Lord. First Corinthians 6:9-10,

> Or do you not know that the unrighteous will not inherit the kingdom of God? Do not be deceived: neither the sexually immoral, nor idolaters, nor adulterers, nor men who practice homosexuality, nor thieves, nor the greedy, nor drunkards, nor revilers, nor swindlers will inherit the kingdom of God.

Greediness competes with purity of life.
Ephesians 4:18-19,

> They are darkened in their understanding, alienated from the life of God because of the ignorance that is in them, due to their hardness of heart. They have become callous and have given themselves up to sensuality, greedy to practice every kind of impurity.

Greediness encourages wickedness.

> **Psalm 37:21** The wicked borrows but does not pay back, but the righteous is generous and gives.

> **Proverbs 15:27** Whoever is greedy for unjust gain troubles his own household, but he who hates bribes will live.

- **Laziness/Sloth/Snail:**

Laziness is attributed to someone who does not like to work, but loves idleness, unwilling to make an effort to change his/her situation.

Laziness is the spirit of the snail. When you try to rebuke or correct a person who has the spirit and symptoms of laziness, he or she will quickly withdraw into a shell of excuses and will refuse to make further attempt to work.

Other words for laziness include: idleness, lethargy, indolence, languor, sluggishness. All these words basically mean the same thing as refusing to use energy and wasting away from fulfillment and advancement of life.

- Laziness does attract procrastination, whereby one keeps postponing an assignment until the time expires.
- Laziness has been described as one of the deadly sins that destroy a person's destiny and relationship with the Lord.

Remez Sasson (www.successconsciousness.com) recommends twelve ways to overcome laziness. Some of his suggestions are included in the following:

1. **Small Units**: Break down a task into smaller units.
2. **Rest**: Rest, sleep and exercise.
3. **Motivation**: Motivate yourself by focusing on achieving goals at certain times.
4. **Goals**: Set goals for your aspirations and write down your expectations.
5. **Obstacles**: Think about the benefits of your proposed goals instead of the obstacles that discourage.
6. **Consequences**: Consider the consequences of not waking up to meet your goals.
7. **Step by Step**: Do one thing at a time. Avoid doing too many things at a time. It will make you feel tired and beclouded.
8. **Inspire Your Thoughts**: Try to visualize what you intend to do and how to do it better.
9. **Speak to Yourself**: Encourage yourself by speaking to your own soul and body as though you are addressing someone you love.
10. **Strengthen Yourself**: Start to see yourself as a leader and an achiever. Give yourself a second chance for a better day.
11. **Celebrate Your Effort**: Make yourself happy at work. Sing songs of joy and celebration. Try to laugh when you make mistakes.
12. **Association**: Relate to people who talk positively about their expectations and how they overcome. Avoid

people who talk loosely to discourage other people from succeeding.

Scripture warns against the characteristics of laziness as sin and destroyer of destiny. A person who is lazy is referred to as a sluggard because it is sluggish and dull in behavior.

> **Proverbs 15:19** The way of a sluggard is like a hedge of thorns, but the path of the upright is a level highway.

Proverbs 6:1-5,

> My son, if you have put up security for your neighbor,
> have given your pledge for a stranger,
> if you are snared in the words of your mouth,
> caught in the words of your mouth,
> then do this, my son, and save yourself,
> for you have come into the hand of your neighbor:
> go, hasten, and plead urgently with your neighbor.
> Give your eyes no sleep and your eyelids no slumber;
> save yourself like a gazelle from the hand of
> the hunter,
> like a bird from the hand of the fowler.

Spirit of an Achiever/Goal Getter

An ant is a goal getter that aims to achieve, no matter the height that it needs to climb. **Proverbs 6:6-8,**

> *Go to the ant, O sluggard;*
> *consider her ways, and be wise.*
> *Without having any chief,*
> *officer, or ruler,*
> *she prepares her bread in summer*
> *and gathers her food in harvest.*

Spirit of Procrastination

The spirit of procrastination makes you lazy and unable to establish yourself in the realm of success. Poverty is like a robber, and want is like an armed bandit that takes away the opportunities of the benefit meant for you. **Proverbs 6:9-11,**

> How long will you lie there, O sluggard?
> When will you arise from your sleep?
> A little sleep, a little slumber,
> a little folding of the hands to rest,
> *and poverty will come upon you like a robber, and want*
> *like an armed man.*

Laziness produces worthlessness. A worthless person turns out to be a crook who exhibits wickedness. **Proverbs 6:12-15,**

> A worthless person, a wicked man,
> goes about with crooked speech,
> winks with his eyes, signals with his feet,
> points with his finger,
> with perverted heart devises evil,
> continually sowing discord;
> therefore calamity will come upon him suddenly;
> in a moment he will be broken beyond healing.

How to Preserve Your Life in Righteousness:

- Father gives the command
- Mother teaches utilization of the command

Proverbs 6:20-22

> My son, keep your *father's commandment*,
> and forsake not your *mother's teaching*.
> *Bind them on your heart always;*

tie them around your neck.
When you walk, they will lead you;
when you lie down, they will watch over you;
and when you awake, they will talk with you.

Proverbs 21:25 The desire of the sluggard kills him, for his hands refuse to labor.

A lazy person is comparable to a fool:

Proverbs 26:1-12,

> Like snow in summer or rain in harvest,
> so honor is not fitting for a fool.
> Like a sparrow in its flitting, like a swallow in
> its flying,
> a curse that is causeless does not alight.
> A whip for the horse, a bridle for the donkey,
> and a rod for the back of fools.
> Answer not a fool according to his folly,
> lest you be like him yourself.
> Answer a fool according to his folly,
> lest he be wise in his own eyes.
> Whoever sends a message by the hand of a fool
> cuts off his own feet and drinks violence.
> Like a lame man's legs, which hang useless,
> is a proverb in the mouth of fools.
> Like one who binds the stone in the sling
> is one who gives honor to a fool.
> Like a thorn that goes up into the hand of a drunkard
> is a proverb in the mouth of fools.
> Like an archer who wounds everyone
> is one who hires a passing fool or drunkard.
> Like a dog that returns to his vomit

is a fool who repeats his folly.
Do you see a man who is wise in his own eyes?
There is more hope for a fool than for him.

The lazy wastes time and energy:

A lazy attitude is storage for poverty.

Proverbs 26:13-16,

> *The sluggard says, "There is a lion in the road!*
> *There is a lion in the streets!"*
> As a door turns on its hinges,
> so does a sluggard on his bed.
> The sluggard buries his hand in the dish;
> it wears him out to bring it back to his mouth.
> *The sluggard is wiser in his own eyes than seven men*
> *who can answer sensibly.*

A lazy person is a waster.

Proverbs 18:9 Whoever is slack in his work is a brother to him who destroys.

A lazy person is a slave to debt.

Proverbs 12:24 The hand of the diligent will rule, while the slothful will be put to forced labor.

The future of a lazy man is bleak.

Proverbs 20:4 The sluggard does not plow in the autumn; he will seek at harvest and have nothing.

- ## Deception/Lying

The practice of misleading somebody with a false information. It is a deliberate act of tricking or cheating with a pretext that the matter is genuine.

- It is fraudulent behavior whereby a person dabbles into double-dealing.
- It is a trick or manipulation that is used to acquire a property, money, or anything.

Other words: dishonesty, trickery, ruse, sham, fraud, cheating, deceit, pretext.

Lying is to make a false statement with the intention to cause someone to believe something.

- Lying is also an attempt to influence someone to do something that they would not usually want to do or be a part of. The act of lying can be verbal or non-verbal.
- A verbal lie is when it is orally committed.
- A non-verbal lie is acted in behavior or attitude.
- Silence can also be an exhibition of a lie.

Proverbs 26:17-23,

Whoever meddles in a quarrel not his own
is like one who takes a passing dog by the ears.
Like a madman who throws firebrands, arrows, and death
is the man who deceives his neighbor
and says, "I am only joking!"
For lack of wood the fire goes out,
and where there is no whisperer, quarreling ceases.
As charcoal to hot embers and wood to fire,
so is a quarrelsome man for kindling strife.
The words of a whisperer are like delicious morsels;

they go down into the inner parts of the body.
Like the glaze covering an earthen vessel
are fervent lips with an evil heart.

• **Pride/Peacock**

On a general note, pride is fundamentally associated with Satan. To describe someone as being proud is to associate the person with Lucifer the fallen archangel who attempted to overthrow the kingdom of righteousness out of envy and jealousy.

Pride has been described as the initial sin that Satan used to entice mankind in the Garden of Eden when he stated in **Genesis 3:1-5,**

> "Did God actually say, *'You shall not eat of any tree in the garden'?"* And the woman said to the serpent, "We may eat of the fruit of the trees in the garden, but God said, 'You shall not eat of the fruit of the tree that is in the midst of the garden, neither shall you touch it, lest you die.'" But the serpent said to the woman, *"You will not surely die. For God knows that when you eat of it your eyes will be opened, and you will be like God, knowing good and evil."*

The Lord's response to pride is punishment.

> **Isaiah 13:11** I will punish the world for its evil, and the wicked for their iniquity; I will put an end to the pomp of the arrogant, and lay low the pompous pride of the ruthless.

> **Isaiah 16:6** We have heard of the pride of Moab— how proud he is!— of his arrogance, his pride, and his insolence; in his idle boasting he is not right.

Isaiah 23:9 The LORD of hosts has purposed it, to defile the pompous pride of all glory, to dishonor all the honored of the earth.

Isaiah 25:11 And he will spread out his hands in the midst of it as a swimmer spreads his hands out to swim, but the LORD will lay low his pompous pride together with the skill of his hands.

1 John 2:16 For all that is in the world—the desires of the flesh and the desires of the eyes and pride of life—is not from the Father but is from the world.

Characteristics of Pride
Inward Emotional feelings:

- Vainglory
- Vanity
- Conceit
- Egotism
- Easily offends
- Inflation of self above others
- Superiority complex
- Deep pleasure
- Satisfaction
- Achievement
- Accomplishment

Characteristics of Peacock

The peacock is one of the graceful birds that are the most beautiful among all other birds. It is the largest flying bird with a large wingspan and train. Its wings are made of attractive pheasant colors that are typically blue and green. It is also known as peafowl. The male is known as the peacock while the female is known as a peahen, and the little ones are referred to as the peachicks.

The peacock is a bird with an ostentatious/flamboyant appearance. It is gorgeous and bluish. Its attractive bright colors are meant for sexual charm to excite the female counterparts. "Sexual selection is the ability of male and female organisms to exert selective forces on each other with regard to mating activity" (www.wikipedia.com).

The female peahen is a "drab, mottled brown in comparison" to the male peacock brightness. The female is usually dull brown and grey in color with short feathers. "The female needs to be able to blend in with the bushes so that predators cannot see her while she is incubating her eggs" (www.kids. sandiegozoo.org).

The peacock is a symbol of pride.

In certain religions the peafowl is adored and worshipped because of its beauty. The peafowl is symbolized with:
Nobility

- Holiness
- Guidance
- Watchfulness
- Protection
- Royalty
- Compassion

The Peafowl in Christianity

In Christianity, the peafowl represents immorality and vanity. Certain schools of thought see the bird as competing with the resurrection of Christ Jesus from the dead.

The peafowl bird sheds its feathers every year for a replacement of a new brighter and thicker one. The multitude of eyes upon its gorgeous fan tail is characterized as the "all seeing" beyond its environment—"the vault of heaven and the eyes of the stars." Likewise, the Lord appeared with power and brightness during his resurrection. The Lord is all knowing and all seeing but beyond the ability and characteristics accorded to the peafowl bird.

There are different kinds of pride. Pride can be negative, positive, or achievement oriented.

Negative Pride: Negative pride is one of the deadly sins that formed the characteristics of Satan. The sin of pride is an evil spirit that transformed Lucifer from being an anointed cherub of God into Satan the devil—the evil one. Originally, Lucifer was "seal of perfection, full of wisdom, and perfect in beauty." The sin of pride turned him into the Father of Lies, the ruler of hell, which is a place of his condemnation.

Ezekiel 28:12-19,

> "Son of man, raise a lamentation over the king of Tyre, and say to him, Thus says the Lord GOD:
> "You were the signet of perfection, full of wisdom and perfect in beauty.
> You were in Eden, the garden of God;
> every precious stone was your covering, sardius, topaz, and diamond,
> beryl, onyx, and jasper,
> sapphire, emerald, and carbuncle;
> and crafted in gold were your settings and your engravings.
> On the day that you were created they were prepared.
> You were an anointed guardian cherub.
> I placed you; you were on the holy mountain of God;
> in the midst of the stones of fire you walked.
> You were blameless in your ways
> from the day you were created,

till unrighteousness was found in you.
In the abundance of your trade
you were filled with violence in your midst, and
you sinned;
so I cast you as a profane thing from the mountain of God,
and I destroyed you, O guardian cherub,
from the midst of the stones of fire.
Your heart was proud because of your beauty;
you corrupted your wisdom for the sake of your
splendor.
I cast you to the ground;
I exposed you before kings, to feast their eyes on you.
By the multitude of your iniquities,
in the unrighteousness of your trade
you profaned your sanctuaries;
so I brought fire out from your midst;
it consumed you,
and I turned you to ashes on the earth
in the sight of all who saw you.
All who know you among the peoples
are appalled at you;
you have come to a dreadful end
and shall be no more forever."

Job 35:12 There they cry out, but he does not answer, because of the *pride of evil men*.

Psalm 10:4 In *the pride of his face* the wicked does not seek him; all his thoughts are, "There is no God."

Psalm 31:18 Let the lying lips be mute, which speak insolently against the righteous in *pride and contempt*.

> **Psalm 31:23** Love the LORD, all you his saints! The LORD preserves the faithful but abundantly repays the one who acts in pride.

According to St. Augustine of Hippo (354-430 A.D), "Pride is the commencement of all sin because it was this which overthrew the devil, from whom arose the origin of sin; and afterwards, when his malice and envy pursued man, who was yet standing in his uprightness, it subverted him in the same way in which he himself fell. For the serpent, in fact, only sought for the door of pride whereby to enter when he said, 'Ye shall be as gods'" (www.allaboutgod.com).

- Negative pride is the feeling of superiority over other people. It is when someone feels better than other people, especially without justification.
- Negative pride is an exhibition of arrogance, conceit, smugness, and self-importance.
- Negative pride is self-centered, and produces high self-respect, self-esteem and it is all about "me, myself, and I."

Scriptures relating to pride include:

> **Psalm 47:4** He chose our heritage for us, the pride of Jacob whom he loves. Selah.

> **Psalm 59:12** For the sin of their mouths, the words of their lips, let them be trapped in their pride. For the cursing and lies that they utter.

> **Psalm 73:6** Therefore pride is their necklace; violence covers them as a garment.

Proverbs 8:13 The fear of the LORD is hatred of evil. Pride and arrogance and the way of evil and perverted speech I hate.

Proverbs 11:2 When pride comes, then comes disgrace, but with the humble is wisdom.

Proverbs 16:18 Pride goes before destruction, and a haughty spirit before a fall.

Proverbs 21:24 "Scoffer" is the name of the arrogant, haughty man who acts with arrogant pride.

Proverbs 29:23 One's pride will bring him low, but he who is lowly in spirit will obtain honor.

Jeremiah 49:16

The horror you inspire has deceived you,
and the pride of your heart,
you who live in the clefts of the rock,
who hold the height of the hill.
Though you make your nest as high as the eagle's,
I will bring you down from there, declares the LORD.

Boasting: It is an expression of pride whereby a person overemphasizes his or her possessions or accomplishments.

Obadiah 1:3 The pride of your heart has deceived you, you who live in the clefts of the rock, in your lofty dwelling, who say in your heart, "Who will bring me down to the ground?"

Mark 7:22-23 Coveting, wickedness, deceit, sensuality, envy, slander, pride, foolishness. All these evil things come from within, and they defile a person.

Positive Pride: Positive pride is to be proud of a particular skill, quality, and/or performance.

- It is to congratulate oneself over an achievement.
- It is to take pride in doing something that many people struggle with.

Other expression for positive pride may include dignity and honor. Sometimes self-respect and self-esteem may be positive if one's intention is discipline oriented.

> **Psalm 47:4** He chose our heritage for us, the pride of Jacob whom he loves. Selah.

> **Isaiah 4:2** In that day the branch of the LORD shall be beautiful and glorious, and the fruit of the land shall be the pride and honor of the survivors of Israel.

> **1 Corinthians 15:31** I protest, brothers, by my pride in you, which I have in Christ Jesus our Lord, I die every day!

> **Colossians 7:4** I am acting with great boldness toward you; I have great pride in you; I am filled with comfort. In all our affliction, I am overflowing with joy.

Achievement Pride: Achievement pride is to place value on someone's efforts, life, or achievement. It is a feeling of deep pleasure that brings joy, peace and satisfaction. Although achievement pride is related to positive expressions, it can also be turned into a sinful behavior if care is not taken and a heart is not properly guarded.

Achievement pride can be described as an experience of satisfaction, pleasure, delight, fulfillment, and gratification.

- It is a quality of life and/or possession.
- It is an admiration of success, victory, and fulfillment.
- It is one of the best conditions that one holds on to in life.
- It is a personal satisfaction obtained from hard work.
- It is an accomplishment of one's aspirations.
- It is a heroic stage of life.
- It is an honor and recognition of performance and achievement.

- **Adultery /Sexual Immorality**

Adultery is a relationship between a married person and someone else who is not the spouse. Adultery is also referred to as sexual immorality when a married person relates to any other person with deep expressions that demonstrate love affairs or romance in secret and/or in public.

Scripture states that when a married person looks at a woman with an expression of sexual longings, it is attributed to the sin of adultery. **Mark 10:5-12 (KJV)**,

> And Jesus answered and said unto them, *For the hardness of your heart he wrote you this precept.* But *from the beginning of the creation God made them male and female. For this cause shall a man leave his father and mother, and cleave to his wife; And they twain shall be one flesh: so then they are no more twain, but one flesh. What therefore God hath joined together, let not man put asunder.* And in the house his disciples asked him again of the same *matter.*

> And he saith unto them, *Whosoever shall put away his wife, and marry another, committeth adultery against her.* And if a woman shall put away her husband, and be married to another, *she committeth adultery.*

Infidelity: It is an act of unfaithfulness and disloyalty in a married relationship. If a married man is a close friend of yours, make sure to draw the wife also close to your heart; otherwise you will be accused and judged with the sin of adultery, which is tantamount to sexual perversion.

The fact that the so-called "celebrity ministers" are divorcing because of their lustful sexual passions does not mean the Lord approves of them. Scripture clearly states that adulterers will not inherit the kingdom of righteousness. It is not about how big or beautiful the fellowship auditorium is, and it is not about how attractive or loquacious the minister may be on the stage; the Word of God remains the same yesterday, today, and forever. Technology cannot and will not change who God is when it comes to righteousness and holiness. The attributes of God are not on the compromising lane of any type of lifestyle. The other day I heard a celebrity minister say that "God is no longer interested in people's marital decisions, so divorce is no longer a big deal." Wow! This is scary and sounds like he is an agent of Satan in charge of divorce. He is in ministry to sway people from the righteous path into perversion. We need to be careful whom we listen to and adore as our spiritual mentor.

> **Jeremiah 23:10 (KJV)** *For the land is full of adulterers; for because of swearing the land mourneth;* the pleasant places of the wilderness are dried up, and their course is evil, and their force is not right.

1 Corinthians 6:9 (KJV) Know ye not that *the unrighteous shall not inherit the kingdom of God? Be not deceived: neither fornicators, nor idolaters, nor adulterers,* nor effeminate, nor abusers of themselves with mankind,

Hebrews 13:4 (KJV) Marriage is honourable in all, and the bed undefiled: but whoremongers and *adulterers God will judge.*

James 4:4 (KJV) *Ye adulterers and adulter-esses, know ye not that the friendship of the world is enmity with God?* whosoever therefore will be a friend of the world is the enemy of God.

Betrayal: To give confidential information about someone to an enemy or a rival. It is also an act of revealing secrets by breaking the trust that has been confided in someone.

Betrayal of trust is to give away the trust that has been invested in you. These include:

- All the secrets things that go on in a marital relationship
- The weaknesses and shortfalls of one's spouse

The Ten Commandments warned in **Exodus 20:14**, "**You shall not commit adultery.**"

Divorce is Deadly

Adultery at any level is unfaithfulness and deceitfulness. Anyone involved in intercessory prayer should not indulge in the act of adultery.

- Adultery kills a marital home and the children inherit the curse of divorce.

- Divorce is the death of a marriage.
- God hates adultery and divorce.
- Divorce is an evil spirit that stands against the institution of marriage.
- Marriage is the first institution that God established in the beginning of creation.
- Anything that interferes with a marital relationship is evil and deadly.

Matthew 19:3-9,

> And Pharisees came up to him and tested him by asking, "*Is it lawful to divorce one's wife for any cause?*" He answered, "Have you not read that he who created them from the beginning made them male and female, and said, '*Therefore a man shall leave his father and his mother and hold fast to his wife, and the two shall become one flesh'*? So they are no longer two but one flesh. What therefore God has joined together, let not man separate." They said to him, "Why then did Moses command one to give a certificate of divorce and to send her away?" He said to them, "*Because of your hardness of heart Moses allowed you to divorce your wives, but from the beginning it was not so.* And I say to you: *whoever divorces his wife, except for sexual immorality, and marries another, commits adultery.*" The disciples said to him, "If such is the case of a man with his wife, it is better not to marry."

How to Preserve Your Life from Perversion/Immorality: **Proverbs 6:23-29**,

> *For the commandment is a lamp and the teaching a light,*

and the reproofs of discipline are the way of life,
to preserve you from the evil woman,
from the smooth tongue of the adulteress.
Do not desire her beauty in your heart,
and do not let her capture you with her eyelashes;
for the price of a prostitute is only a loaf of bread,
but a married woman hunts down a precious life.
Can a man carry fire next to his chest
and his clothes not be burned?
Or can one walk on hot coals
and his feet not be scorched?
So is he who goes in to his neighbor's wife;
none who touches her will go unpunished.

Adultery Is Stealing:

- The sin of adultery is stealing.
- It destroys a person's destiny.
- It is an opposition to the scriptural Word of God, the Ten Commandments.

Proverbs 6:30-35,

People do not despise a thief if he steals
to satisfy his appetite when he is hungry,
but if he is caught, he will pay sevenfold;
he will give all the goods of his house.
He who commits adultery lacks sense;
he who does it destroys himself.
He will get wounds and dishonor,
and his disgrace will not be wiped away.
For jealousy makes a man furious,
and he will not spare when he takes revenge.
He will accept no compensation;
he will refuse though you multiply gifts.

- **Fornication /Impurity**

Fornication is a sexual affair between two single people (a bachelor and a spinster) who are not married to each other. Both adultery and fornication are related in meaning to sexual affairs out of wedlock. Adultery and fornication is the state where two persons relate to one another on illegal grounds as though they are married but are not.

Just like the case of adultery, fornication is a spirit of impurity that opens doors to the enemy to enter into an environment of intercessory prayer. Fornication is an evil spirit that causes shame and disgrace to come upon a person in order to defile the purity of an altar where godly activities are performed.

The term *fornication* is also translated idolatry and whoredom in the Hebrew Old Testament. **2**

Chronicles 21:10-14,

So Edom revolted from the rule of Judah to this day. At that time Libnah also revolted from his rule, because he had forsaken the LORD, the God of his fathers. Moreover, he made high places in the hill country of Judah and led the inhabitants of Jerusalem into whoredom and made Judah go astray. And a letter came to him from Elijah the prophet, saying, "Thus says the LORD, the God of David your father, 'Because you have not walked in the ways of Jehoshaphat your father, or in the ways of Asa king of Judah, but have walked in the way of the kings of Israel and have enticed Judah and the inhabitants of Jerusalem into whoredom, as the house of Ahab led Israel into whoredom, and also you have killed your brothers, of your father's house, who were better than you, behold, *the LORD will bring a great plague on your people, your*

> *children, your wives, and all your possessions,*
> *and you yourself will have a severe sickness*
> *with a disease of your bowels, until your bowels*
> *come out because of the disease, day by day.'"*

In the New Testament, "fornication" comes from the Greek word porneia, which includes adultery and incest. Porneia comes from another Greek word that also includes indulging in any kind of unlawful lust, which would include homosexuality. The use of the word in the gospels and the epistles is always in reference to sexual sin, whereas "fornication" in the book of Revelation always refers to idolatry. The Lord Jesus condemns two of the churches of Asia Minor for dabbling in the fornication of idolatry. **Revelation 2:14-20**,

> But I have a few things against you: you have some there who hold the teaching of Balaam, who taught Balak to put a stumbling block before the sons of Israel, so that they might *eat food sacrificed to idols and practice sexual immorality.* So also you have some who hold the teaching of the Nicolaitans. Therefore repent. If not, I will come to you soon and *war against them with the sword of my mouth.* He who has an ear, let him hear what the Spirit says to the churches. To the one who conquers I will give some of the hidden manna, and I will give him a white stone, with a new name written on the stone that no one knows except the one who receives it.' "And to the angel of the church in Thyatira write: 'The words of the Son of God, who has eyes like a flame of fire, and whose feet are like burnished bronze. "*I know your works, your love and faith and service and patient endurance, and that your latter works exceed the first. But I have this against you, that you*

> *tolerate that woman Jezebel, who calls herself*
> *a prophetess and is teaching and seducing my*
> *servants to practice sexual immorality and to*
> *eat food sacrificed to idols.*

Christ Jesus referred to "the great harlot" of the end times, which is the idolatrous false religion "with whom the kings of the earth committed fornication, and the inhabitants of the earth were made drunk with the wine of her fornication." **Revelation 17:1-2,**

> Then one of the seven angels who had the seven
> bowls came and said to me, "Come, I will show
> you the judgment of the great prostitute who is
> seated on many waters, with whom the kings
> of the earth have committed sexual immorality,
> and with the wine of whose sexual immorality
> the dwellers on earth have become drunk."

- **Uncleanness /Sensuality:**

Sensuality is the pursuit and expression of sexual pleasure outside of marriage. It is a seductive behavior whereby someone has no control over a passion for evil desires. Sensuality leads to sexual passion and eventually to a reprobate mind. **Romans 1:21-23,**

> For although they knew God, they did not honor
> him as God or give thanks to him, but they
> became futile in their thinking, and their foolish
> hearts were darkened. Claiming to be wise, they
> became fools, and exchanged the glory of the
> immortal God for images resembling mortal
> man and birds and animals and creeping things.

Sensuality is a longing for the sinful desires of the flesh. It is an uncontrollable response to satisfy the urges of the sensory organ in the flesh. It is a war against the fruit of the Spirit of God. **Galatians 5:16** says, "But I say, walk by the Spirit, and you will not gratify the desires of the flesh."

Sensuality is the cause of indulgence in pornography, lust of the eyes, lust of the flesh, excessive desire for material things, vanity lifestyle, wasteful spending, and such like. **1 John 2:15-17**,

> *Do not love the world or the things in the world.* If anyone loves the world, the love of the Father is not in him. *For all that is in the world—the desires of the flesh and the desires of the eyes and pride of life—is not from the Father but is from the world.* And the world is passing away along with its desires, but whoever does the will of God abides forever. (ESV *Emphasis added*).

- **Lasciviousness /Idolatry**

Lasciviousness is a behavior that is driven by sexual thought and desire.

Mark 7:21-23

> 21 For from within, out of the heart of men, proceed evil thoughts, adulteries, fornications, murders,
>
> 22 thefts, covetousness, wickedness, deceit, lasciviousness, an evil eye, blasphemy, pride, foolishness:

23 All these evil things pass out from inside and defile the man.

- It is an attempt to advertise one's sexual desires.
- It is to make known one's sexual intention publicly.
- It is a carnal action.
- It is an ungodly thought.
- It is a public indecency.
- It is an excessive sensuality that has no shame.
- It is an indecent expose of the body's nakedness to a crowd.
- It is an indecent maneuvering of body to entice the opposite gender or same sex.
- It is unchaste and indecent handling of a male or female.
- It is uncontrollable sexual appetite.

Romans 13:12-14

12 The night *is* far spent, the day is at hand; therefore let us cast off the works of darkness, and let us put on the armor of light.

13 Let us walk becomingly, as in *the* day; not in carousings and drinking; not in co-habitation and lustful acts; not in strife and envy.

14 But put on the Lord Jesus Christ, and do not take thought beforehand for the lusts of the flesh.

2 Corinthians 12:20-21

20 For I fear, lest somehow coming I might not find you as I wish, and *that* I shall be found by you such as you might not wish; lest somehow *there be* strifes, envyings, angers,

contentions, backbitings, whisperings, proud thoughts, tumults;

21 lest in my coming again my God will humble me with you; and I shall mourn many who have already sinned, and not repenting over the uncleanness, and fornication, and lustfulness which they have practiced.

Others words for lasciviousness are:

* Lustfulness
* Lewdness
* Sexy
* Libidinous

Galatians 5:16-19

16 I say, then, Walk in *the* Spirit and you shall not fulfill *the* lusts of *the* flesh.

17 For the flesh lusts against the Spirit, and the Spirit against the flesh. And these are contrary to one another; lest whatever you may will, these things you do.

18 But if you are led by *the* Spirit, you are not under law.

19 Now the works of the flesh are clearly revealed, which are: adultery, fornication, uncleanness, lustfulness,

20 idolatry, sorcery, hatreds, fightings, jealousies, angers, rivalries, divisions, heresies,

21 envyings, murders, drunkennesses, revelings, and things like these; of which I tell you before, as I also said before, that they who do such things shall not inherit the kingdom of God.

Recent indulgences in lasciviousness include:

* Pornography
* Flirtation and Extra-marital Affairs
* Fornication and Adultery

Ephesians 4:17-19

17 This I say therefore, and testify in *the* Lord, that you should not walk from now on as other nations walk, in *the* vanity of their mind,

18 having the understanding darkened, being alienated *from* the life of God through the ignorance that is in them, because of the blindness of their heart.

19 For they, being past feeling, have given themselves up to lust, to work all uncleanness with greediness.

I Peter 4:1-3

1 Therefore, Christ having suffered for us in *the* flesh, also you arm yourselves *with* the same thought, that he suffering in *the* flesh has been made to rest from sin,

2 in order no longer to *live* in *the* lusts of men, but in *the* will of God the remaining time in *the* flesh.

3 For the time of life which is past is enough for us to have worked out the will of the nations, having gone on in lasciviousness, lusts, excess of wine, parties, carousings, and abominable idolatries.

2 Peter 2:6-8

6 And turning the cities *of* Sodom and Gomorrah into ashes, He condemned *them* with an overthrow, setting an example to *men* intending to live ungodly.

7 And He delivered righteous Lot, oppressed with the lustful behavior of the lawless.

8 For that righteous one living among them, in seeing and hearing, *his* righteous soul *was* tormented from day to day with *their* unlawful deeds.

2 Peter 2:18

17 These are wells without water, clouds driven with a tempest, for whom the blackness of darkness is reserved forever.

18 For when they speak great swelling *words* of vanity, they lure through *the* lusts of the flesh, by unbridled lust, the ones who were escaping from those who live in error;

19 promising them liberty, they themselves are the slaves of corruption. For by whom anyone has been overcome, even to this one he has been enslaved.

Jude 1:4 For certain men crept in secretly, those having been of old previously written into this condemnation, ungodly ones perverting the grace of our God for unbridled lust, and denying the only Master, God, even our Lord Jesus Christ.

- **Witchcraft /Sorcery**

Witchcraft is a kind of seductive charm that is used to lure and influence other people with the use of demonic powers. It is also a manipulative and controlling power that is used for casting a spell, suppressing and oppressing people at will. It is a kind of magical power that depends on the forces of darkness to subdue people in order to achieve its aim.

Witchcraft is a type of evil spirit. A possessor of the spirit may be conscious or unconscious of its presence in his or her life. A conscious witch deliberately invokes the powers of darkness to do evil against other people. An unconscious witchcraft possessor will usually seek help for freedom.

A male that possesses a witchcraft spirit is a wizard or sorcerer. A female that possesses the spirit is a witch. There are different types of witchcraft practices such as:

- Necromancy
- Palmistry
- Voodoo
- Divination
- Magic
- Baalism

- Ashtoreth
- Medium
- Spiritualism
- Horoscope
- Eastern Meditation Rituals
- Ouija Board

Revelation 22:15,

Outside are the dogs and sorcerers and the sexually immoral and murderers and idolaters, and everyone who loves and practices falsehood.

Witchcraft is one of the dangerous practices that could easily contaminate the environment of intercessory prayer. It is an opening to witchcraft activities. The act of witchcraft is a contentious spirit that likes to compete with the works and presence of the Holy Spirit. Both conscious and unconscious witches may want to dominate and control the environment of prayer with false revelation to distract the prayer activities. Witches could manipulate the leaders with deceptive requests where there is no discerning of spirits.

Witchcraft Prayers

Certain dangerous prayers that are being uttered by some Christians are demonic utterances that cast spells on fellow Christians to bewitch them.

In recent times, many Christians are adopting satanic ritualism and incantation into their prayers. While Scripture admonishes us to overcome evil with good, Christians are praying against one another—calling fire to consume brothers and sisters who have offended them. Many are misusing the power and authority in the blood of Jesus as a weapon to destroy souls that need to be saved from perishing. **Isaiah 57:1-5,**

The righteous man perishes,
and no one lays it to heart;
devout men are taken away,
while no one understands.
For the righteous man is taken away from calamity; he
enters into peace;
they rest in their beds
who walk in their uprightness. But you, *draw near,
sons of the sorceress,
offspring of the adulterer and the loose woman.* Whom
are you mocking?
Against whom do you open your mouth wide
and stick out your tongue?
Are you not children of transgression, the offspring of
deceit, *you who burn with lust among the oaks,
under every green tree,
who slaughter your children in the valleys,
under the clefts of the rocks?*

Elijah called on fire to consume satanic practices, not fellow prophets. Ministers are praying against one another's ministries. Some people are breaking down denominational churches and stealing sheep and goats to form their own kingdom.

The questions are:

1. Who can draw souls into the kingdom of God by practicing witchcraft and saying demonic incantation?
2. Who is qualified to determine who goes to heaven by building human kingdoms out of strife, hatred, envy, and jealousy?
3. How can we draw souls to Christ and into the kingdom of God if we keep making utterances to destroy one another?

4. What is the essence of the shedding of the blood and reconciliation of man to God through the death of Jesus Christ on the cross?

Hey everybody, take note of these facts:

- The fact that people claim to pray in the name of Jesus does not mean they have the right motive.
- The fact that people are using the blood of Jesus to offer and make incantations does not mean they have access to the Lord.
- The fact that someone quotes the Scriptures to lure people or get attention does not mean they are Christians.

Listen to this:

I have always heard confessions from people who were agents of Satanism. Some of them acting as agents of darkness were actively involved in various church activities to deceive and contaminate soft-minded people.

- The agents of darkness and practitioners of witchcraft acted as though they were committed and dedicated to the church.
- They gave generously to contaminate the offering and the source of income.
- They control and manipulate church authorities and leadership to frustrate divine assignments.

God warned the children of Israel against all manner of witchcraft practices. **Deuteronomy 18:9-12**,

> When you come into the land that the LORD your God is giving you, you shall not learn to follow the abominable practices of those

nations. There shall not be found among you anyone who burns his son or his daughter as an offering, anyone who practices divination or tells fortunes or interprets omens, or a sorcerer or a charmer or a medium or a necromancer or one who inquires of the dead, for whoever does these things is an abomination to the LORD. And because of these abominations the LORD your God is driving them out before you.

Saul consulted the mediums.

1 Samuel 15:23 For rebellion is as the sin of divination, and presumption is as iniquity and idolatry. Because you have rejected the word of the LORD, he has also rejected you from being king."

1 Samuel 28:7-9,

Then Saul said to his servants, "Seek out for me a woman who is a medium, that I may go to her and inquire of her." And his servants said to him, *"Behold, there is a medium at En-dor."* So Saul disguised himself and put on other garments and went, he and two men with him. *And they came to the woman by night.* And he said, "Divine for me by a spirit and bring up for me whomever I shall name to you." The woman said to him, "Surely you know what Saul has done, how *he has cut off the mediums and the necromancers from the land.* Why then are you laying a trap for my life to bring about my death?"

Pharaoh's magicians contended with Moses

Exodus 8:7 But the magicians did the same by their secret arts and made frogs come up on the land of Egypt.

You can be like God: The serpent beguiled the woman in the Garden of Eden by telling her that she would be like God if she should eat from the forbidden tree. Hence, the women yielded and that led to the disobedience and fall of mankind.

> **Genesis 3:5** For God knows that when you eat of it *your eyes will be opened, and you will be like God*, knowing good and evil."

Revelation 18:23

> And the light of a lamp
> will shine in you no more,
> and the voice of bridegroom and bride
> will be heard in you no more,
> for your merchants were the great ones of the earth,
> and *all nations were deceived by your sorcery.*

Characteristics of Practitioners of Witchcraft Include:

- Excessive desire for power and authority
- Usurpation of authority
- Control and manipulation
- Insubordination to authority
- Expression of pride and ego
- Rebelliousness and stubbornness
- Disregard for the Word of God
- Uplifting human revelation above the Scripture
- Considering human prophecy as superior over the legal Word of God
- Self-willed and holding on to sensual passions and worldly desires

- Rejection of Scriptural truth.

These characteristics can also be found in people who are actively involved in church work, and yet are not submissive to authority or are living and walking in disobedience to the Word of God. Usually, excessive desire for power and authority can make a Christian leader or minister to indulge in witchcraft activities.

> **Isaiah 47:12** Stand fast in your enchantments and your many sorceries, with which you have labored from your youth; perhaps you may be able to succeed; perhaps you may inspire terror.

> **John 8:44-45** You are of your father the devil, *and your will is to do your father's desires.* He was a murderer from the beginning, and does not stand in the truth, because there is no truth in him. *When he lies, he speaks out of his own character, for he is a liar and the father of lies.* But because I tell the truth, you do not believe me.

> **James 3:15** This is not the wisdom that comes down from above, *but is earthly, unspiritual, demonic.*

> **Acts 8:9-11** But there was a man named Simon, *who had previously practiced magic* in the city and amazed the people of Samaria, saying that he himself was somebody great. They all paid attention to him, from the least to the greatest, saying, "This man is the power of God that is called Great." *And they paid attention to him because for a long time he had amazed them with his magic.*

Jeremiah 5:23 But this people has a stubborn and rebellious heart; they have turned aside and gone away.

- **Hatred and Enmity:**
Proverbs 26:24-28

Whoever hates disguises himself with his lips
and harbors deceit in his heart;
when he speaks graciously, believe him not,
for there are seven abominations in his heart;
though his hatred be covered with deception,
his wickedness will be exposed in the assembly.
Whoever digs a pit will fall into it,
and a stone will come back on him who starts it rolling.
A lying tongue hates its victims,
and a flattering mouth works ruin.

- **Wrath/Fits of Anger/Lion:**

Proverbs 15:1-3,

A soft answer turns away wrath,
but a harsh word stirs up anger.
The tongue of the wise commends knowledge,
but the mouths of fools pour out folly.
The eyes of the LORD are in every place,
keeping watch on the evil and the good.

- Strife /Rivalries/ Variance:
- Seditions /Dissensions:
- Heresies/Divisions:
- Murders/Murders:
- Drunkenness/Drunkenness:
- Revelings/Orgies:

Summary

Access: Intercessors are usually highly gifted people who have the opportunity to see and know from the past to the present. The revelatory gifts also make them prophetic to a certain extent because intercession gives them a unique access into the courtroom of heaven. Like an attorney, they go into different chambers of the court for different reasons depending on their assignment.

Contempt of Court: However, an attorney may be found illegal and charged with contempt of God because of misbehavior due to lack of knowledge and lack of integrity. An attorney who has no integrity may lose his or her license and is barred from practice and from the court chambers. Such is the case of an intercessor that has no moral integrity and indulges in character assassination.

False Burden: An intercessor who does not demonstrate the fear of God in character and behavior may be found wanting as he or she could be involved in betrayal of trust and unfaithfulness. If the person does not quickly seek repentance for restoration, very much the spirit of intercession will no longer operate in the person's life. The person's connection with the realms of intercession would be severed because sin blocks a person from hearing the Lord directly. If care is not taken, the spirit of lies will take over and the person will begin to carry a false burden and will operate with deception.

Intercession in Action

Prayer Focus
Need wisdom against intercessory pitfalls

Goal
Need to understand the dangers of intercessory pitfalls
Need to guard against lack of uprightness in times of dangers
and perils of battlefields
Need to be alert and sensitive against the snare of the fowler
Need to be diligent to resist the noisome pestilence of sin that
frustrates
intercessory prayer
Need to be steadfast and fervent in righteous living against
the trap of the enemy
Need to be consistent to abiding in the word of the Lord
against the lure of the enemy

Prayer of Worship and Adoration
O Lord God our Lord and Maker,
The great and awesome God,
The Covenant-Keeping God,
Whose steadfast love never ceases,
The God who watches over His commandments,
O Lord, let your ears be attentive to our cry.
And hear the cry of our hearts,
As we call upon you day and night.

Prayer of Confession and Repentance
O Lord, listen to the confession of our sins,
Which we have sinned against you,
Forgive us our trespasses,
As our fathers and mothers of many generations
Have transgressed your word
by committing grievous sins against your commandments.
We have acted corruptly against you

And have not kept your commandments,
The statutes, and the rules according to your written word.
O Lord, remember your word that states in 1 John 1:9 that,
"If confess our sins, you are faithful and just to forgive us
of our sins and to cleanse us from all unrighteousness."
O Lord, please forgive us our sins,
And restore us unto yourself.

Prayer of Forgiveness and Restoration
O Lord, remember your word in Joel 2:12-13 that also
states that
"Yet even now," declares the LORD,
"return to me with all your heart,
with fasting, with weeping, and with mourning;
and rend your hearts and not your garments."
Return to the LORD your God,
for he is gracious and merciful,
slow to anger, and abounding in steadfast love;
and he relents over disaster.
O Lord, forgive and remove the affliction of sin out of
our lives,
According to your written word in Joel 2:20 that says,
"But I will remove far off from you the northern *army*,
and will drive him into a land barren and desolate,
with his face toward the east sea,
and his hinder part toward the utmost sea,
and his stink shall come up, and his ill savour shall come up,
because he hath done great things."
O Lord, remember your promise for restoration
according to Joel 2:19,
"The LORD answered and said to his people,
'Behold, I am sending to you
grain, wine, and oil,
and you will be satisfied;
and I will no more make you
a reproach among the nations.'"

Invocation of Blessing:

O Lord my God, I ask that you bless me with
Your supernatural image in which you created me.
Pour out your Spirit upon me
To exhibit your likeness in all my endeavors.
O Lord, give me a new heart, a new mind,
A new soul, and a new spirit to enable me
To fear you all the days of my life.
Give me a new tongue and language to talk with
the love and fear of your presence and power.
Deliver me from deadly sins and the sins that you hate,
That I may not be cast out of your presence
And perish in unrighteousness.
O Lord, open the floodgates of heaven
And pour out abundance of blessings upon me,
With long life, good health, and prosperity.
Bless and keep me in rich resources
According to your riches in glory. Amen!

Song of Motivation

Jesus Paid It All

Jesus Paid It All
<u>Elvina M. Hall</u>, 1865
Copyright status is <u>*Public Domain*</u>
Subject: Jesus/Savior
Scripture: Isaiah 1:18; I Peter 1:18-19; Revelation 1:5-6

1. I hear the Savior say,
   "Thy strength indeed is small;
   Child of weakness, watch and pray,
   Find in Me thine all in all."

   Refrain:
   Jesus paid it all,
   All to Him I owe;
   Sin had left a crimson stain,
   He washed it white as snow.

2. For nothing good have I
   Whereby Thy grace to claim;
   I'll wash my garments white
   In the blood of Calv'ry's Lamb.

3. And now complete in Him,
   My robe, His righteousness,
   Close sheltered 'neath His side,
   I am divinely blest.

4. Lord, now indeed I find
   Thy pow'r, and Thine alone,
   Can change the *leper's spots [*leopard's]
   And melt the heart of stone.

5. When from my dying bed
   My ransomed soul shall rise,
   "Jesus died my soul to save,"
   Shall rend the vaulted skies.

6. And when before the throne
   I stand in Him complete,
   I'll lay my trophies down,
   All down at Jesus' feet.

*Alternate text, alluding to Jeremiah 13:23

References:

Parrott, W.G. & Smith, R.H. (1993). "Distinguishing the experiences of envy and jealousy." *Journal of Personality and Social Psychology*, 64, 906-920.

www.allaboutgod.com (December 7, 2015)

www.english.stackexchange.com (December 13, 2015)

www.erlc.com

www.deadlysins.com

www.diffen.com (November 27, 2015)

www.huffingtonpost.com

www.library.timelesstruths.org/music/Jesus_Paid_It_All/

www.patheos.com

www.plato.stanford.edu (November 27, 2015)

www.successconsciousness.com.

www.thesaurus.com

www.en.m.wikipedia.org

Bibliography

Grudem, W. (2000). *Systematic Theology: An Introduction to Biblical Doctrine*. Grand Rapids, MI: Zondervan Publishing House.

Parrott, W.G. & Smith, R.H. (1993). "Distinguishing the experiences of envy and jealousy." *Journal of Personality and Social Psychology*, 64, 906-920.

The American Heritage Dictionary of the English Language (5th ed.). (2011). Boston, MA: Houghton Mifflin Harcourt.

www.allaboutgod.com (December 7, 2015)

www.ccg.org

www.BibleResources.org

www.deadlysins.com

www.desiringgod.org

www.dictionary.reference.com

www.diffen.com (November 27, 2015)

www.english.stackexchange.com (December 13, 2015)

www.erlc.com

www.e-sword.com

www.freedictionary.com

www.huffingtonpost.com

www.Merriam-webster.com

www.mysticalblaze.com

www.Nationaldayofprayer.org

www.patheos.com

www.plato.stanford.edu (November 27, 2015)

www.relevantbibleteaching.com

www.Sacred-text.com/cla/tms08.htm

www.successconsciousness.com.

www.thefreedictionary.com

www.thequickenedword.com

www.thesaurus.com

www.vocabulary.com

www.en.m.wikipedia.org

Decision

I f you have never surrendered your life to Jesus Christ, to accept him as your Lord and Savior, then it is important for you to do so right away. Otherwise, it will be difficult for you to conquer the enemy, and to overcome the negative spirits that rule your life. If you are willing to accept Jesus Christ as your Lord and Savior, then pray like this:

> *Lord Jesus, I come to you just as I am.*
> *Forgive my sins and deliver me from all works of iniquity.*
> *Deliver me from all the evil characteristics that affect my life.*
> *Deliver me from all the behaviors that have kept me in bondage.*
> *Set my soul and spirit free to worship you in spirit and in truth.*
> *Come into my life and make me whole.*
> *I need you, Lord.*
> *I need you every hour unto eternity. Amen!*

Rededication

I f you have once made a decision to surrender your life to Christ Jesus, but you have been struggling with the Christian life, then you need to rededicate your life in order to gain a reconnection with the Lord. Also, if you are somehow an active Christian, but are still struggling with some ungodly characteristics and behaviors, then you need to rededicate yourself to the Lordship of Jesus Christ. Make a total surrender, so that the enemy will not have any form of control in your life.

You may pray like this:

> *Lord Jesus, teach me to surrender my total being to your Lordship and control, so that the enemy will no longer have a part in me.*
> *Teach me to abide in you, so that you will also abide in me, and dwell in my life.*
> *O Lord, teach me to study your Word, and to make a conscious effort to apply it to my daily living.*
> *O Lord, wash me, cleanse me, and purify my spirit, soul, and body,*
> *so that I may be acceptable in Your sight.*
> *Thank you, Lord, for delivering me from the works of iniquity. Amen!*

Pauline Walley Deliverance Bible Institute (PWDBI) & Prophetic-Deliverance Theological Training Institute

(School of Intensive Training for Ministry and Leadership Equipment)

The Pauline Walley Deliverance *Bible Institute* is a school of intensive training that equips and empowers leaders, individuals, and church groups in the ministry. It is an intensive, practical training center where people are taught to build their images and personalities, to improve their ministry skills and abilities, develop their talents and gifts, and minister to family members, friends, churches, and/or fellowship members, and to themselves.

In the process of training, people learn how to receive ministration against the battle of life as it is in our daily endeavors.

The areas of study include the following:

- School of Deliverance
- School of Strategic Prayer
- School of Tactical Evangelism
- School of Mentoring and Leadership
- School of the Gifts of the Holy Spirit
- School of the Prophets
- School of Prophetic Deliverance
- School of Prophetic Intercession

- School of Ministerial Responsibilities and Church Administration

The School of Intensive Trainings are held in different parts of the world at various times. At seminar levels, one week, or two weeks of intensive training help leaders and ministers, or church/fellowship groups to establish various arms of church ministry, and equip their members for such purposes.

Biweekly intensive training programs, the one-year certificate course, and degree programs are readily available in the Bronx, New York, and other regions based on request. If you are interested in hosting any of these programs in your region, country, or church/ministry, please contact us. See details about our contact information and web site on the back pages.

Author's Resources

Christian Books
By Dr. Pauline Walley (Dr. Pauline Walley-Daniels)

Deliverance Ministration:

1. Receive and Maintain Your Deliverance
2. Solution: Deliverance Ministration to Self and Others
3. Pulling Down Strongholds
4. When Satan Went to Church
5. Anger: Get Rid of it
6. 3-21 Days Esther Progressive Prayer Fast
7. Strategies Deliverance Solution: Discover and Destroy Ancestral Curses
8. Deliverance Solution Wisdom: Freedom I
9. Deliverance Solution Wisdom: Freedom II
10. Deliverance Solution Wisdom: Release
11. Strategic Deliverance Warfare: Interference
12. Strategic Intercessory Warfare: Weapons

Strategic Prayer Tactics:

13. Strategic Prayer Tactics I
14. Strategic Prayer Tactics II
15. Strategic Prayer Tactics III
16. Destiny Solutions Prayer: Lord Make Me Over
17. Progressive Solution Prayers for Fruitfulness and Fulfillment

Holy Spirit:

18. Holy Spirit: Power of the Tongue
19. Holy Spirit: Uniqueness of His Presence
20. Holy Spirit: Maintain His Presence in Trials and Temptations
21. Holy Spirit: Power of the Spoken Word

Mentoring and Leadership:

22. The Authority of An Overcomer
23. Mentoring and Leadership I: The Art of Mentoring
24. Mentoring and Leadership II: Progressive Achievement
25. Mentoring and Leadership III: Somebody Cares

The Prophetic:

26. School of Prophetic Deliverance
27. Prophetic Preparation Training I
28. Prophetic Preparation Training II

Workbooks: (Workbooks available for all books)

Prophetic Ministry
Deliverance Ministration:
Strategic Prayer
Mentoring and Leadership

Subscription

Gospel Songs on CDs

- "Overcomers' Expression"
- "Send Your Power"
- "Vessels of Worship"
- "Poetic Expression"

BOOKS
All the books listed are available in bookstores, and by order on line.

UNITED STATES
Pauline Walley Christian Communications
P.O. Box 250, Bronx, NY 10467
Tel: (718) 652-2916
Fax: (718) 405-2035
E-mail: admin@paulinewalley.org
Web site: www.school-of-deliverance.com
www.paulinewalley.org
www.paulinewalley.com
www.pwdi.org

About the Book

N o military officer goes to war without weapons. No commander-in-chief sends out a troop of army officers without training them to identify wars and face battles. No officer carries a weapon that he has not been trained to handle. This book on *Strategic Intercessory Warfare: Weapons*, trains you on how to be equipped and empowered through intercessory prayer. It teaches you to understand spiritual communications and also educates you on how to engage the enemy at war and on battlefields. It enlightens you on how to identify the enemy and what kind of weapon is needed for specific warfare. It also enables you to understand the kind of preparation that is needed to confront the enemy at state.

Author's Biography

Pauline Walley-Daniels, PhD, is an ordained prophetic deliverance apostle who teaches the Word of God with dramatic demonstrations. She is the president of Pauline Walley Evangelistic Ministries and Christian Communications, as well as the CEO of the Prophetic Deliverance Theological Training Institute, which includes the School of Intensive Training for Leadership Equipment, and the School of Deliverance in New York.

Dr. Pauline is affiliated with Christian International Ministries Network; Academic Council for Educational Accountability; International Coalition of Apostles; and is the Secretary General of Faith Ministers Fellowship of New York. Dr. Pauline serves on Christian Life Educators Network Board of Regents. She is one of Morris the Cerullo Prayer Strike Force Ministers.

She holds a master's degree in journalism and a PhD in Pulpit Communications and Expository Preaching. Dr. Pauline is the author of several books and is married to Rev. Frederick Daniels of Overcomers' House Prophetic Deliverance Church in the Bronx of New York, USA.

CPSIA information can be obtained
at www.ICGtesting.com
Printed in the USA
BVHW032152180820
586773BV00001B/6

9 781631 298028